Israel
Vision and Reality

Israel
Vision and Reality

Massada | MOD Publishing House

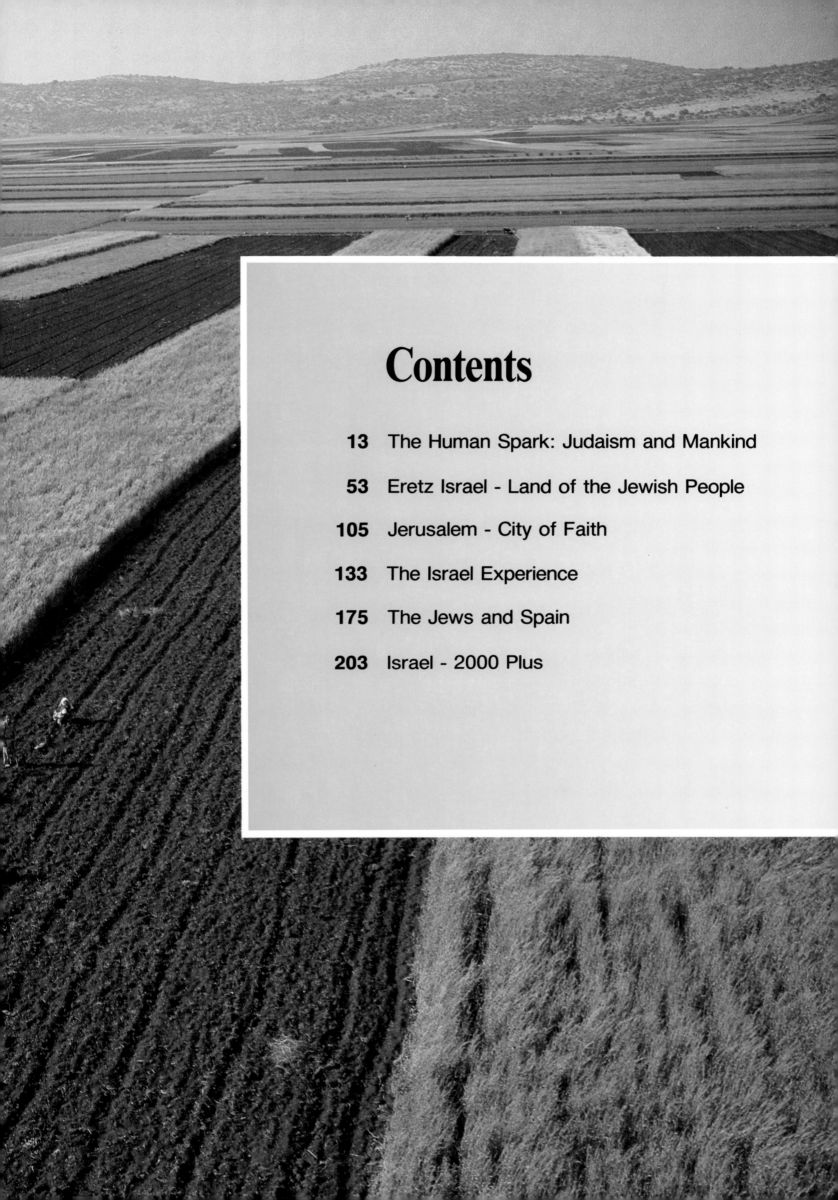

Contents

Written by Amos Carmel
Editorial board: Shalom Seri, Yoav Barash, Shlomo Rosner
Design: Doreet Scharfstein
Picture editors: Shmuel Stempler, Rachel Schnold, Naama Cifrony
Project Coordinator: Ishak Kempler
Production: Joseph Levin, Aharon Frosh

The Jewish genius was marked out by *moral fervor*, which preserved the people when nothing remained of all its neighbors but dim memories or broken sherds. Unlike the sages of other peoples in ancient days, Israel's prophets looked forward to the future, to the 'last days.' They saw the Golden Age not in a distant past, but in the time to come.

They were not content with this vision of political and moral redemption for their own people. They desired freedom and justice not for Jews alone, but for all men – righteousness and peace between the nation.

They were not mystics; they were men of foresight. They gazed deep into the secrets and strivings of humankind.

Our place in the world as a free people will be assured if we help to build a better, juster, kindlier world. Not by wealth, or power, or numbers, but through the example of our lives will we help to spread justice and peace among the nations, and thus alone will we ourselves win peace.

We have it in us to build in the Homeland a Jewish people which men everywhere will laud and emulate – its life, economy, society, culture, and internal and external policies based on the teachings of the Prophets, the lessons of justice, mercy and peace. This is the moral imperative of our past, the imperative of our attachment to Diaspora Jewry, the political imperative of our place in the world. In this vision is the secret of our survival, our resurgence. Where there is no vision, the people perish.

David Ben-Gurion

אנכי יי
לא יהי
לא תשא
זכור את
כבד את

לא תרצח
לא תנאף
לא תגנב
לא תענה
לא תחמד

The Human Spark: Judaism and Mankind

לפרר יב ביקי אדכ מש
לבנ ישרא במשרי
למיאב על יהריאל
ליהרייחול

ציך יהוה ביר משה
אל בני ישראל מעתן
מיאב של יהר דחל
אלה פקריא והריא

ומשיז והוול אחסנתן
על שבטא זרעיה
אמרן אלה המינצה
והמשפטים אש־

דלום קטל קטי מזרנך יהלך ירטשיד והטלטוב
ושמטה ובטל לבהקט ומתטן והיב אטחוב
וטמא יתבאזם זקר שיטתי עשרים אמרלנב
טב

דברים אשר הפר
משה אל כל ישראל
בעפר היריך כמירל
בערבה מיל סיה בן
מאז וצר יפל וכן ולבן
חניית וחי זהב אלי
פארמעיא זמליל מש
שם על ישרא בעברא
 היריא איכב יהרו
על רהכי במיבל א

יאל האדכהו במשרא לה
לקלי ים סיה בפאי
אפטלי על מיצא ובן
בחיז חדה ארהו ש
כיסרא וכל הצבר יה
אלה שטן יכאל
לב בן פנרי זבאל
שיתהטקופו יבה זפרייו פתם עריה
על ושר שאנ על יצא שעלי הופרה
הינתין חי ריב שטהטיכ עזטרהים
חטמיבו כניזנדך בימן וקשמע בזה
 שם יוסי בישרו יקשתן לך כסבם

כילם ויאבו לחם הרו עדכא פולהוא כאן
של גוי שעש לו תעיטה וקשם ברייתי
שא בפיסם חוי עלא בפקטנית כיאב
מרישת שעחבשה בד תוד פיהטבר וכל
בעטל חעצטא שחלאו במל קטי
טעטין גל שעחב ברם סזד פוראם לה
טוריא זמניטל אנך שבים שפיי עטל
כליה מ טזהי ניות חים שפני עטל
וזכ זפל ולבן ־ שט ל הינון חזבי
על אברחתא זלא ברידגר בהיקזת שתין
שטהרא תכטל ולבן ־אלא הקשיאן על
במיט שחטלי בזך שזוויא בזי־שאטבי
טלטים חליהיל זעל בה מיט שעינטי בניהי
ביטלהם ־ של חים מט יזג לאבם
זבר אלכ כלולטין בזבני שענטאים הפן
כחיניא ־ בשעזל אטהין חרע ואדרבמ ב

וְגָרְשֶׁה נָחֲלָתוֹ מִנַּחֲלַת
אֲבַהָתֵיהּ תְּוֹסֵף עַל נַ
נַחֲלָה הַמַּטֶּה אֲשֶׁר
תִּהְיֶינָה לָהֶם וּמִנַּחֲלַת
נָחַלְתַּנָא יָרֵעַ וְאֵיהֶוֹ
לְחַר בְּיֹבֵל שַׁבְטֵי יֵי
יִשְׂרָאֵל לְנַשְׁיֵי וְיִתְנְסַב
אַחֲסַנְתְּהוֹן מֵאֲחַסְנַת
אֲבָהָתְנָא וְיִתְּוֹסַף עַל
אֲחַסְנָה שַׁבְטָא רֵיהּ
דִּיְתֵהוֹי לְהֶן וּמֵעַב
אֲחַסְנָתָנָא יִתְמְנַע

וְאִם יִהְיֶה הַ
לִבְנֵי יִשְׂרָאֵל וְנוֹסְפָה
נָחֲלָתוֹ עַל נַחֲלַת
וּמַשֶּׁה אֲשֶׁר תִּהְיֶינָה
לַהֶם וּמִצְבָהֵל וּמֵשֶׁה
אֲבֹתֵינוּ יֵרַעֵ נָחֲלָתָם
וְאִם יִתֵּי יִוּבְלָא לִבְנֵי
יִשְׂרָאֵל וְיִתְוֹסַף לִבְנֵי
אַחֲסַנְתְּהוֹן עַל אַחֲסַנַת
שַׁבְטָא דִּי יֵהֵוֹי לְהֶן
וּמֵאַחֲסַנַת שַׁבְטֵיהּ
דַּאֲבָהָתָנָא יִתְמְנַע
אֲחֲסָנַתְהֶן וְאִם יְהֵי
יוֹבְלָא לִבְנֵי יִשְׂרָאֵל
שְׁמֵיהּ עֲלֵידֵיהּ שַׁבְטֵי
עֲשֵׁר וְתֵהֵוֹי לְשַׁבְטֵי
רָאֲבַהָתָנָא יִתְמְנַע
אֲחֲסַנְתְּהֶן וְאִם יְהֵי

וַיְצַו מֹשֶׁה
אֶל בְּנֵי יִשְׂרָאֵל עַל
פִּי יְהוָה לֵאמֹר כֵּן
מַשֵּׁה בְנֵי יוֹסֵף דֹּבְרִים

וְעָבַר עַד נַחְלַתְּכֶם בְּנַחֲלַת אֲבֹתֵיכֶם וּנְדַבֵּק נַחֲלָה עַל נָחֲלָה הַטּוֹבָה אֲשֶׁר הַתִּי וַהַבְנֵי לַהֶם כֵּי הֵהֵיה הַבֵּל לִבְנֵי יִשְׂרָאֵל וַנֹּסֵף נַחֲלָה עַל נַחֲלָה
אֲשֶׁר וְדָיְבַק לָהֶם וַנַּחֲלָה וּנְבֵטֵלָה בְּיוֹם הַכִּלָּה כֵּי יְהוָה דָּבַר כֵּן מֹשֶׁה בֵּן יוֹסֵף כֵּן נְדַבֵּר אֲשֶׁר יֵהֵיה וְלֹא תִסֹּב נַחֲלָה לְבָנֵי יִשְׂרָאֵל וְתֵהֵיה כְנַחֲלָה שֵׁבוֹת
וֵיִלְבַבֵּר לְאִמֹר לֵטוֹרָים טַעַ יֶטֶרֶם הַהֵי עַד לְמִשְׁפַּחַת מֵה תִהְיֶה אַךְ לְמִשְׁפַּחָה כֵּן נַחֲלָה לִבְנֵי יִשְׂרָאֵל אֲל מַטֶּה אֲל מַטֶּה כֵּי אֵשׁ בְּנַחֲלָתוֹ יוֹם

בארץ-ישראל קם העם היהודי, בה עוצבה דמותו הרוחנית, הדתית והמדינית, בה חי חיי קוממיות ממלכתית, בה יצר נכסי תרבות לאומיים וכלל-אנושיים והוריש לעולם כולו את ספר הספרים הנצחי.

לאחר שהוגלה העם מארצו בכוח הזרוע שמר לה אמונים בכל ארצות פזוריו, ולא חדל מתפלה ומתקוה לשוב לארצו ולחדש בתוכה את חירותו המדינית.

מתוך קשר היסטורי ומסורתי זה חתרו היהודים בכל דור לשוב ולהאחז במולדתם העתיקה, ובדורות האחרונים שבו לארצם בהמונים, וחלוצים מעפילים וגגינים הפריחו נשמות, החיו שפתם העברית, בנו כפרים וערים, והקימו ישוב גדל והולך השליט על משקו ותרבותו, שוחר שלום ומגן על עצמו, מביא ברכת הקדמה לכל תושבי הארץ ונושא נפשו לעצמאות ממלכתית.

בשנת תרנ״ז (1897) נתכנס הקונגרס הציוני לקול קריאתו של הוגה חזון המדינה היהודית תיאודור הרצל והכריז על זכות העם היהודי לתקומה לאומית בארצו.

זכות זו הוכרה בהצהרת בלפור מיום ב בנובמבר 1917 ואושרה במנדט מטעם חבר הלאומים, אשר נתן במיוחד תוקף בין-לאומי לקשר ההיסטורי שבין העם היהודי לבין ארץ-ישראל ולזכות העם היהודי להקים מחדש את ביתו הלאומי.

השואה שנתחוללה על עם ישראל בזמן האחרון, בה הוכרעו לטבח מיליונים יהודים באירופה, הוכיחה מחדש את ההכרח בפתרון בעית העם היהודי מחוסר המולדת והעצמאות על ידי חידוש המדינה היהודית בארץ-ישראל, אשר תפתח לרווחה את שערי המולדת לכל יהודי ותעניק לעם היהודי מעמד של אומה שוות-זכויות בתוך משפחת העמים.

שארית הפליטה שניצלה מהטבח הנאצי האיום באירופה ויהודי ארצות אחרות לא חדלו להעפיל לארץ-ישראל, על אף כל קושי, מניעה וסכנה, ולא פסקו לתבוע את זכותם לחיי כבוד, חירות ועמל-ישרים במולדת עמם.

במלחמת העולם השניה תרם הישוב העברי בארץ את מלוא-חלקו למאבק האומות השוחרות חירות ושלום נגד כוחות הרשע הנאצי, ובדם חייליו ובמאמצו המלחמתי קנה לו את הזכות להמנות עם העמים מייסדי ברית האומות המאוחדות.

ב-29 בנובמבר 1947 קבלה עצרת האומות המאוחדות החלטה המחייבת הקמת מדינה יהודית בארץ-ישראל, העצרת תבעה מאת תושבי ארץ-ישראל לאחוז בעצמם בכל הצעדים הנדרשים מצדם הם לביצוע ההחלטה. הכרה זו של האומות המאוחדות בזכות העם היהודי להקים את מדינתו אינה ניתנת להשקעה.

זוהי זכותו הטבעית של העם היהודי להיות ככל עם ועם עומד ברשותו עצמו בדינתו הריבונית.

לפיכך נתכנסנו, אנו חברי מועצת העם, נציגי הישוב העברי והתנועה הציונית, ביום סיום המנדט הבריטי על ארץ-ישראל ובתוקף זכותנו הטבעית וההיסטורית ועל יסוד החלטת עצרת האומות המאוחדות אנו מכריזים בזאת על הקמת מדינה יהודית בארץ-ישראל, היא מדינת ישראל.

אנו קובעים שהחל מרגע סיום המנדט, הלילה, אור ליום שבת ו אייר תש״ח, 15 במאי 1948, ועד להקמת השלטונות הנבחרים והסדירים של המדינה בהתאם לחוקה שתיקבע על-ידי האספה המכוננת הנבחרת לא יאוחר מ׳א באוקטובר 1948 – תפעל מועצת העם כמועצת מדינה זמנית, ומוסד הביצוע שלה, מנהלת-העם, יהווה את הממשלה הזמנית של המדינה היהודית, אשר תקרא בשם י ש ר א ל.

מדינת ישראל תהא פתוחה לעליה יהודית ולקיבוץ גלויות; תשקוד על פיתוח הארץ לטובת כל תושביה; תהא מושתתה על יסודות החירות, הצדק והשלום לאור חזונם של נביאי ישראל; תקיים שויון זכויות חברתי ומדיני גמור לכל אזרחיה בלי הבדל דת, גזע ומין; תבטיח חופש דת, מצפון, לשון, חינוך ותרבות; תשמור על המקומות הקדושים של כל הדתות; ותהיה נאמנה לעקרונותיה של מגילת האומות המאוחדות.

מדינת ישראל תהא מוכנה לשתף פעולה עם המוסדות והנציגים של האומות המאוחדות בהגשמת החלטת העצרת מיום 29 בנובמבר 1947 ותפעל להקמת האחדות הכלכלית של ארץ-ישראל בשלמותה.

אנו קוראים לאומות המאוחדות לתת יד לעם היהודי בבנין מדינתו ולקבל את מדינת ישראל לתוך משפחת העמים.

אנו קוראים – גם בתוך התקפת-הדמים הנערכת עלינו זה חדשים – לבני העם הערבי תושבי מדינת ישראל לשמור על השלום וליטול חלקם בבנין המדינה על יסוד אזרחות מלאה ושווה ועל יסוד נציגות מתאימה בכל מוסדותיה, הזמניים והקבועים.

אנו מושיטים יד שלום ושכנות טובה לכל המדינות השכנות ועמיהן, וקוראים להם לשיתוף פעולה ועזרה הדדית עם העם העברי העצמאי בארצו. מדינת ישראל מוכנה לתרום חלקה במאמץ משותף לקדמת המזרח התיכון כולו.

אנו קוראים אל העם היהודי בכל התפוצות להתלכד סביב הישוב בעליה ובבנין ולעמוד לימינו במערכה הגדולה על הגשמת שאיפת הדורות לגאולת ישראל.

מתוך בטחון בצור ישראל הננו חותמים בחתימת ידינו לעדות על הכרזה זו, במושב מועצת המדינה הזמנית, על אדמת המולדת, בעיר תל-אביב, היום הזה, ערב שבת ה אייר תש״ח, 14 במאי 1948.

"**Eretz Israel** is the birthplace of the Jewish people. Here their spiritual, religious and political identity was shaped. Here they first attained statehood, created cultural values of national and universal significance and gave the world the eternal Book of Books."

It is with these words that the Declaration of Independence of the State of Israel opens, words which proclaimed on the 14th of May 1948 that the Jews were returning to renew their full sovereignty in their historical homeland, and which, at that historic moment, gave clear expression not only to the place of the Jews in the family of nations but also to the lasting significance of the prime document that articulates this people's tie to the land – the eternal Book of Books, the Bible.

The Bible is the Book of Books even in the simplest technical sense. Every bibliotheca, every bibliography, every bibliophile must hark back to a source which is called the Bible. But civilized people also know that the Bible is the Book of Books in the fullest sense of the words. This ancient work, preserved and sanctified over thousands of years, is one of the world's greatest spiritual treasures. In content and form it prescribes criteria of conduct for all of mankind, but, encapsulating the history of the Jewish people, it is the fundamental pillar of the Jewish faith, culture and language. It is this which made the Jews into "the People of the Book," and it is this which went forth from Judaism to the world at large, becoming a cornerstone of western culture in its many different guises.

The Bible begins with a concise description of the creation of the world and the shaping of mankind through Adam's decision to eat from the Tree of Knowledge. Immediately afterwards we have the story of Abraham, "the father of a multitude of nations" and of the Jewish people. The Bible does not teach us exactly what caused the dramatic transformation in Abraham's life, how a Mesopotamian shepherd became the founder of monotheism. Talmudic legend, though, tells how Terah, Abraham's father, made idols for a living, and how Abraham, in charge of selling them, realized their worthlessness and smashed them. In the Bible itself we are only told that Abraham at the age of seventy-five hears a command from above, from the One God, who has no physical form or substance, "Go from your country and your kindred and from your father's house to the land which I will show you. And I will make you into a great nation ... and through you all the families of the earth will be blessed." And Abraham listens and obeys.

He cuts himself off from his previous roots, as befits the father of a major revolution, goes down to the southern border of the Fertile Crescent, and comes to rest in that area which later will come to be known as the Land of Israel, a land named after one of his grandsons. Here he again has a divine revelation, in which God makes a covenant with him, and it is here that he pleads to God on behalf of the people of Sodom, begging that a handful of righteous men not be destroyed along with the wicked. Here he undergoes the terrible test of the sacrifice of Isaac, his only son, whom he loves, and learns that his new faith does not favor human sacrifice. Here, in his travels and trials, in his struggles with his enemies on the one hand and his feelings on the other, contending with the tribulations of the environment, Abraham begets his nation and creates a tradition which will be handed down to all of his descendants.

Let my people go

Abraham's grandson and great-grandsons are forced to descend to Egypt because times are so difficult, and the account of their departure from that land, after four hundred years of slavery there, is also part of the Bible. Indeed, its central element is the motif of national liberty – the struggle to attain freedom from those who would enslave others, and the striving for national freedom – which was to become a universal symbol for all of mankind. Moses the stutterer, the

The fourth day of the Creation, according to the Old Testament and as seen by a German artist before 1250. (right).

The sacrifice of Isaac as depicted in the mosaic pavement, (below), of the sixth century C.E. synagogue found in 1929 at Beit Alpha in the Valley of Jezreel.

man who throughout the generations has so fascinated thinkers and artists, the prophet and legislator, who alone, we are told, "God knew face to face," goes out to his brethren in their backbreaking work and witnesses their suffering. Then he raises the banner of rebellion both against the brutal tyranny of Pharaoh and the servility of the

19

The mountains of Sinai: it was in this vicinity that, seven weeks after their Exodus from Egypt, Moses took the Children of Israel to meet with God. (Below: The Children of Israel leaving Egypt, as seen by a 15th century illustrator of a Passover Haggadah printed in Nuremberg, Germany.)

Opposite: The Sinai scene as depicted in an illustrated Old Testament from the 14th century.

Israelites. Later he will oppose the longing for the flesh pots of Egypt and the worship of the golden calf. With his call, "Let my people go," that is to become the rallying cry of all those throughout history and the world who seek freedom, he leads the Children of Israel out of Egypt – but not immediately into the Promised Land. First they must make their way into the desert, where their character can be refined so that they can shake off their slave mentality and become a nation worthy of sovereignty.

Moses leads the Children of Israel to the slopes of Mount Sinai for the giving of the Torah, the Pentateuch, whose core is the Ten Commandments. Those who had left Egypt only seven weeks earlier, who had suddenly become free men, who were wrested from their persecutors, are now given a

code the likes of which was unknown anywhere in the ancient world:

"...You shall not make for yourself an idol or graven image of any thing that is in the heavens above or that is on the earth below or that is in the waters under the earth. You shall not bow down to them nor worship them, because I am the Lord your God...

You shall not take the name of the Lord your God in vain, because the Lord will not hold blameless he who takes His name in vain.

Remember the Sabbath day to keep it holy ... You shall not do any work, neither you, nor your son, nor your daughter, nor your manservant, nor your maidservant, nor your cattle, nor the stranger who is within your gates ...

Honor your father and your mother ...

You shall not murder.

You shall not commit adultery.

You shall not steal.

You shall not bear false witness against your neighbor.

You shall not covet ..."

Thus was created the infrastructure for the conceptual system and the norms of Judaism and Western culture. It began with a series of verses based on the Ten Commandments and became the basis for the ethos of human progress and social justice to this day. A random

22

selection of these verses speaks for itself:

"You shall not persecute the stranger nor oppress him, because you were strangers in the land of Egypt. You shall not oppress any widow or orphan."

"If you lend money to ... the poor who is with you, you shall not be to him as a lender of money, nor shall you lay usury upon him."

"You shall not follow a multitude to do evil; neither shall you give perverse testimony in a dispute to pervert it in favor of the mighty, nor shall you show deference to a poor man in his dispute."

"If you see your enemy's donkey falling under its load ... you shall surely unload with him."

"You shall not take bribes, because bribery blinds the eyes of the wise and perverts the words of the righteous."

"When you sell a thing to your fellow or buy from your fellow's hand, you shall not cheat one another."

"The land shall not be sold in perpetuity."

"If your fellow waxes poor and falls down by you, you shall take hold of him, both the stranger and resident, and he shall live with you."

"You shall set up judges and officers in all your gates ... and they shall judge the people justly."

"Justice, justice shall you pursue, that you may live."

"You shall destroy evil from your midst."

"You shall not shift your fellow's border."

"When you draw near to a city to wage battle against it, you shall call to it for peace."

"You shall not return a slave to his master, if he took refuge with you from his master."

"Fathers shall not be killed for sons and sons shall not be killed for their fathers; each man shall be killed for his own sin."

"You shall not have in your houses measure and measure, large and small ... You shall have a full and proper measure."

The True Prophets

Equipped with these principles, along with rules which translated them into daily laws of social justice and a denial of arbitrary decisions, the Children of Israel returned to their land, settled it, struggled for their existence and for their freedom and anointed their first king, Saul. He was not of noble stock, not a wealthy man, not a representative of a powerful family, just one of the common folk, a member of the small tribe of Benjamin who had gone out to search for his lost donkeys. "He stood amongst the people" – not above them – "from his shoulders and upward he was taller than any of the people."

Following him as king was a shepherd, who slew the giant Philistine, Goliath, with a stone, and who eventually would become not only a king that expanded his empire by conquest, but also the Sweet Singer of Israel and author of the beautiful Psalms.

It was David, son of Jesse, who taught all of mankind that "The Lord is my shepherd, I shall not want/ He makes me lie down in green pastures/ He leads me beside still waters/ He restores my soul/ He leads me in the paths of righteousness for His name's sake./ Yea, though I walk through the valley of the shadow of death/ I shall fear no evil, for You are with me/ Your rod and Your staff they comfort me./ You prepare a table before me in the presence of my enemies/ You anoint my head with oil, my cup runneth over./ Surely goodness and mercy will follow me all the days of my life/ And I shall dwell in the house of the Lord forever."

It was he who wrote: "Lord, who shall dwell in Your tabernacle/ Who shall dwell in Your holy hill?/ He that walks uprightly and works righteousness, and speaks the truth in his heart/ He that does not backbite with his tongue, nor does evil to his neighbor/ Nor takes up a reproach against neighbor/ In whose eyes a vile person is condemned, but he

honors those who fear the Lord/ He that swears to his own hurt, and changes not/ He that puts not his money out to usury, nor takes reward against the innocent/ He that does these things shall never be moved."

David, King of Israel, was also the father of the dynasty from which, we are told, will emerge the Messiah at the End of Days. Of the Messiah, it is written: "The spirit of the Lord shall rest upon him, the spirit of wisdom and understanding, the spirit of counsel and might, the spirit of knowledge and the fear of the Lord; And shall make him of quick understanding in the fear of the Lord: and he shall not judge after the sight of his eyes, neither reprove after the hearing of his ears: But with righteousness shall he judge the poor, and reprove with equity for the meek of the earth: and he shall smite the earth with the rod of his mouth, and with the breath of his lips shall he slay the wicked. And righteousness shall be the girdle of his loins, and faithfulness the girdle of his reins."

Yet David was a king whose own sins were not forgiven and who possessed no immunity. "You are the man," says the prophet Nathan as he points accusingly at David, after the king had sinned against his servant Uriah. "And now, the

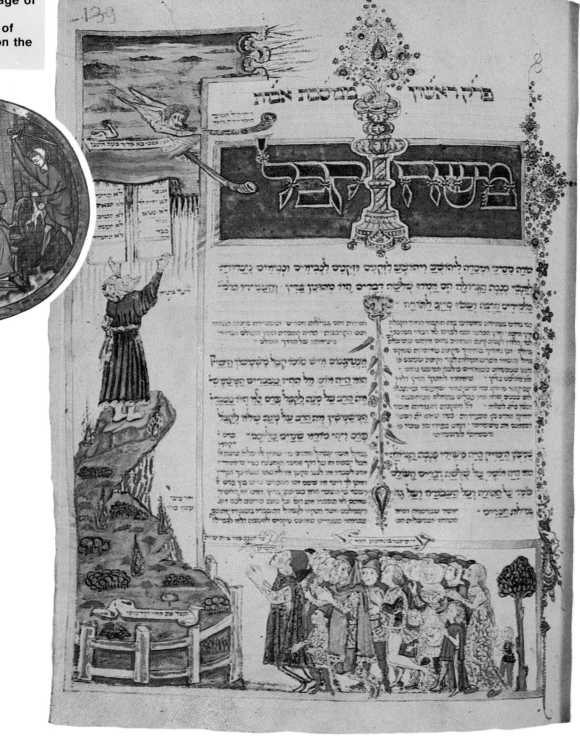

sword will never depart from your house because you have scorned me." And "because you are a man of war and have spilled blood," David was forbidden to build the Temple.

This privilege was granted to his son and heir, Solomon, "the wisest of all men," who asked of God not wealth nor that his enemies be delivered into his hands, but "a discerning heart to judge Your people, to distinguish between good and bad." The Temple which Solomon built on Mount Moriah in Jerusalem became the focal point of Jewish belief. The priests who served in it accumulated much authority, had access to the ruling classes and enjoyed economic stability. Only the High Priest was permitted to enter the Holy of Holies, and then only on the most solemn day of the year, **Yom Kippur**. But the power of the priests declined, to be supplanted by that of the prophets, who were Moses' spiritual heirs.

Even when the Children of Israel had wandered in the desert, they had been told: "I will raise up a prophet among them like you, and I will place My words in his mouth and he will speak to them that which I command him." The true prophets, those who clung to moral ethics and justice, not those who spoke "wantonly" and "in the name of other gods," determined criteria for moral values and proper conduct, not only for their own generation but for future generations. Constantly in opposition to those who abused power, to those who fomented strife throughout the land, fearless critics of corruption, they stressed that man's relationship to his fellow-man takes precedence over his relationship to God.

One such prophet was Elijah, who came from the tiny village of Tishba in the mountains of Gilead to the very seat of power of the Kingdom of Israel, and was not afraid to stand alone against King Ahab and against the 450 prophets of Baal and fight for the truth. It was Elijah who learned, as he dwelled in a cave, that "the Lord was not in the wind ... and the Lord was not in the earthquake ... and the Lord was not in the fire; and afterwards there was a still, small voice." And it was Elijah who railed against the king, "Did you then murder and also inherit?" and who promised him, "I will bring evil upon you, and take away your posterity."

Another great prophet, one of the first whose works were committed to writing, was Isaiah the son of Amotz, who prophesied in Jerusalem for 45 years in the eighth century

The Prophet Elijah sometime in the ninth century B.C.E., berated the King Ahab for pagan ways and laxity – and asked him a crucial question: "Did you then murder and also inherit?" Elijah's name is connected with many legends. One, illustrated on the right by a painting of the 14th century Russian Nizni Novgorod school, is about how he dwelt by the brook, Cherith, and how ravens brought him bread and meat. There is the dramatic story of Elijah confronting 450 prophets of Baal on Mount Carmel (opposite) – today on the spot where that meeting might have taken place there is a Carmelite monastery with a statue of Elijah in its garden (insert).

B.C.E. When he stood up before the inhabitants of this city, he informed them in the name of God: "To what purpose is the multitude of your sacrifices unto me? ... Your new moons and your appointed feasts my soul hates, they are a trouble unto me; I am weary to bear them. And when you spread forth your hands, I will hide My eyes from you; yea, when you make many prayers, I will not hear; your hands are full of blood. Wash you, make you clean; put away the evil of your doings from before My eyes; cease to do evil ... seek judgment, relieve the oppressed, judge the fatherless, plead for the widow ... Zion will be redeemed with justice, and those who return to it with righteousness."

Isaiah also prophesied about the eternal peace of the End of Days, the era when "the mountain of the Lord's house shall be established on the top of the mountains, and shall be exalted above the hills; and all nations shall flow unto it. And many people shall go and say, 'Come you, and let us go up to the mountain of the Lord, to the house of the God of Jacob; and he will teach us of His ways, and we will walk in His paths.' For out of Zion shall go forth the Torah, and the word of the Lord from Jerusalem. He shall judge among the nations, and shall rebuke many people; and they shall beat their swords into plowshares, and their spears into pruninghooks; nation shall not lift up sword against nation, neither shall they learn war any more."

The great prophet Isaiah Ben Amotz, born in Jerusalem about 765 B.C., delivered a message of days to come when "nation shall not lift up sword against nation; neither shall they learn war any more". Among the Dead Sea Scrolls, there is one complete Book of Isaiah scroll (above).

Isaiah's vision of a time when man and nature at last live in harmony serves in modern times as inspiration for the designers of Israeli stamps (insert).

Another prophet, Amos, who testified that "I am not a prophet nor the son of a prophet but a herdsman and a gatherer of sycamore fruit," thundered from Beth-El, against "the cows of Bashan who are on Mount Samaria, who oppress the poor, who crush the destitute," and cried out against "the three transgressions of Israel, and for four, I will not turn away the punishment thereof – because they sold the righteous for silver, and the poor for a pair of shoes." He adds, "Though you offer Me burnt offerings and your meal offerings, I will not accept them; neither will I regard the peace offerings of your fat beasts. Take you away from Me the noise of your songs; for I will not hear the melody of your viols. But let justice run down as waters, and righteousness as a mighty stream ... Hear this, O you that swallow up the needy, even to make the poor of the land to fail ... making the ephah small and the shekel great, and falsifying the balances by deceit ... Shall not the land tremble for this, and every one mourn that dwells therein?"

Other giants of Hebrew prophecy were Jeremiah (who declared: "If you thoroughly amend your ways and your doings, if you thoroughly execute judgment between a man and his neighbor, if you oppress not the stranger, the fatherless, and the widow, and shed not innocent blood in this place, neither walk after other gods to your hurt, then will I cause you to dwell in this place, in the land that I gave to your fathers, for ever and ever") and Micah (who cried out: "Hear this, I pray you, you heads of the house of Jacob, and princes of the house of Israel, that abhor justice and pervert all equity. They build up Zion with blood and Jerusalem with iniquity. Their heads judge for reward, and

the priests thereof teach for hire, and the prophets thereof divine for money ... Therefore shall Zion for your sake be plowed as a field, and Jerusalem shall become heaps, and the mountain of the house as the high places of the forest."). Others, Ezekiel and Jonah, Joel and Hosea among them, God-driven prophets and men of vision "of exalted spirit," in the words of the Zionist thinker Ahad Ha'am, rose up "upon the borders of nations and states and preached justice and charity to all mankind," preaching that their nation should be – again in the words of Ahad Ha'am -"a single, whole nation, which from generation to generation, without a break, would be a perpetual unique bearer of the power of justice as opposed to all the other forces prevalent in the world."

In the Bible we also find Ecclesiastes, who reminds us that "I perceive that there is nothing better than that a man should rejoice in his own works, for that is his portion: for who shall bring him to see what shall be after him?" And "two are better than one; because they have a good reward for their labor," and "the patient in spirit is better than the proud in spirit." In the pages of the Bible we also encounter the afflictions

31

suffered by Job and his doubts ("What is my strength, that I should hope? and what is my end, that I should prolong my life?"), and the lovely love song of the Song of Songs ("I charge you, O you daughters of Jerusalem, by the roes, and by the hinds of the field, that you stir not up, nor awake my love, till he please").

People of the Book

In the wake of these scriptures, there would arise in the Second Temple era a great sage known as Hillel the Elder, who reduced the entire Torah – with all its philosophy and commandments – to a single principle: "That which is hateful to you do not do unto your fellow. That is the entire Torah. The rest is commentary – go, study." It may well be because of statements such as this that future sages would rule that in the case of a dispute, "the law is in accordance with the School of Hillel."

The Jewish diaspora was created after the destruction of the First Temple (in 586 B.C.E.). For the first few hundred years it was concentrated primarily in the Middle East, and contributed, among others, to the building of bridges between the Jews and other nations. Prominent in this regard was Alexandrian Jewry, whose most famous son was

The Song of Songs (above) which appears towards the end of the Old Testament, is a love song whose lines are permeated with the sights and scents of spring in Eretz Israel.

"Love thy neighbour as thyself" – this early declaration of the rights of man appears in the Talmud. This brings to mind yet another Israeli stamp (Below).

the philosopher Philo (in Hebrew, his name was Yedidya), who drew from Plato and the Stoics and sought to mediate between Judaism and Greek philosophy.

It was in this community that, from the beginning of the 3rd century B.C.E., the monumental work of the translation of the entire Bible into another language – in this case, Greek – was undertaken, yielding the Septuagint. The word itself means "seventy," an allusion to the legend that seventy Jewish scholars were consigned to separate rooms to translate the Bible, and that all presented the identical text, as the result of divine intervention. The final product shows it was faithful to the original in terms of content, form and grammatical structure. The entire venture was apparently conceived to supply the needs of Jews who spoke Greek, but its main result was in spreading the Bible throughout the civilized world of those days and the introduction of its verses and ideas to western civilization.

This translation, which would be followed by translations into many other languages, also meshes with the story of the development of Christianity and its drawing upon Jewish sources, something which would also be important in the development of another great monotheistic religion, Islam. Yet, as these two religions expanded throughout the world, the Jews would be forced to withdraw inward, to their own

home, as it were, and there to utilize their great creative talents for hundreds of years.

Following the destruction of the Second Temple (70 C.E.) and the terrible crushing of the Bar-Kochba rebellion (135 C.E.), Jewish sovereignty in the Land of Israel came to an end. But the spiritual center of the Jews in Eretz Israel continued to function. In the midst of the Roman siege of Jerusalem, Rabbi Yohanan ben Zakkai approached the Roman general, Vespasian, and asked for – and was granted – Yavne (Jabneh) and its sages. There, and afterwards elsewhere in the country, the other basic texts of Judaism – the Mishnah and the Talmud – were formulated. It is these which would accompany the nation in its long exile, shaping its life style and ensuring its existence as a single collective being for hundreds of years. This collective would spread throughout the entire world, the links between its various segments sometimes stronger and sometimes weaker. Now and then it would lose entire segments and here and there, enjoy accretions by conversion. But its existence would never be terminated.

It was an existence made subject to most stringent constraints. The Jews would have to struggle again and again not only for their right to cling to their religion but, first and foremost, for their very lives. Often engulfed by seas of profound hatred, they would be killed for their faith and because they were different. They would become the object of suspicion and false accusations, be limited in their choice of occupations, be hunted until death, and be forced to live in segregated sealed quarters.

One of these quarters was set up in the 16th century in the Italian city of Venice, near a foundry which the local residents called the "ghetto," and thereafter the name would be applied to the Jewish quarters of many cities throughout the Diaspora. But the ghettos and other concentrations of Jewish life were centers of intense activity, in which the flame of knowledge burned unceasingly. More than that – the collective existence within them faithfully reflected the "People of the Book." During hundreds of years of exile and tribulation, the Jews lived with their books and according to their books, transmitting them from generation to generation, sharpening minds and thoughts on them. They established for themselves leaders who were scholars of the Holy Books, partly because the other arenas of human endeavor

In the 16th century the Jews of Venice were restricted to live in a small quarter near a foundry called the "ghetto". Thereafter the name would be applied to the Jewish quarters of many cities. Opposite: a picturesque scene of the first ghetto and the magnificent interior of one of its synagoges.

were closed to them. And everything, or almost everything, was internal – maintained within the four cubits of the community, with little involvement in the lives and culture of the outside world.

They preserved a tradition. They showed an ability to withstand calamity and to survive which must be regarded with admiration. But they were prevented from taking major steps outside their own milieu, from discovering continents, forging new styles of art, building cities, finding new sea routes, changing the economy or waging wars. And yet, here and there there were brilliant lights which shone beyond the ghetto walls, and now and again men appeared whose contributions were deeply imprinted – even in times of the Jews' greatest hardships – on society outside.

Notable among these personalities was Maimonides, Moses the son of Maimon (1138-1204), the man dubbed "the Great Eagle," of whom it was said, "From Moses (i.e., the Lawgiver) until Moses (Maimonides) there never arose such as Moses." Maimonides was the greatest authority in Jewish law of all generations, an important philosopher, astronomer, legal expert and famed doctor, the leader of the Jewish community in Egypt. Born in Cordoba, Spain, he wandered with his family, at first in Spain, afterwards in Morocco and in the Land of Israel, finally settling in Cairo, where he became court doctor in Saladin's court. First he wrote the monumental *Mishneh Torah*, offering a comprehensive code of all Jewish laws, based on a survey of the vast corpus of works on the subject. Afterwards he wrote his great *Guide for the Perplexed*, in which he attempted to reconcile the principles of Jewish religious belief with Aristotelian philosophy and a rational explanation of the laws of nature. The **Guide**, translated into Latin at the beginning of the 13th century as well as into most European languages, influenced a long list of western philosophers over the course of centuries.

Maimonides' eleven medical treatises were also highly influential. Among others, they offer a description of psychosomatic manifestations, a correct assessment of the side effects of various medicines and descriptions of surgical procedures. Written in Arabic, they were translated into

Maimonides, Rabbi Moses Ben-Maimon (above) – one of the greatest of all Jewish scholars, Cordoba-born author of "Mishneh Torah", a monumental code of all Jewish laws (right, an illustrated 14th century manuscript) and of the controversial "Guide for the Perplexed" in which he sought to prove that reason and faith were both sources of revelation.

Hebrew and Latin and were used extensively by doctors in the Middle Ages.

Following in the footsteps of Maimonides was Rabbi Levi ben Gershon (Geisonides – 1288-1344), a philosopher, Bible commentator, physician, mathematician and astronomer, who lived in today's France. His first work was *Sefer Ha-Mispar – The Book of the Number* – in which he dealt with mathematical principles and their applications, and in which, independently, he developed important trigonometrical theorems. His most important work was *Sefer Milhamot Adonai (The Book of the Battles of the Lord)* – which is divided into six sections dealing with the immortality of the soul, prophecy, God's all-encompassing knowledge and man's free will, divine providence, the celestial spheres and the creation of the world. In the philosophical sections of the treatise, Geisonides is revealed as an Aristotelian thinker who does not limit himself to the religious sphere and does not hesitate to come out against either Maimonides or Aristotle. In its astronomical section, he criticizes the Ptolemaic system and introduces two major innovations: a geometric model to calculate the movement of the moon and Jacob's Staff – a device to determine the angle between various heavenly bodies, which served as a navigational instrument utilized by many seafarers.

Jacob's staff, a nautical instrument, for navigation, was developed by a Jewish scholar, Levi Ben Gershon (1288-1344) who lived in what is today France and was a noted philosopher, Biblical commentator, physician, mathematician and astronomer.

Geisonides' philosophical views had profound positive and negative effects on Baruch (Benedict) Spinoza (1632-1677), one of the major figures in the intellectual history of the western world and the most important philosopher to arise among the Jews. Georg Hegel said about him: "Either Spinoza or no philosophy at all." Henri Bergson gave expression to his greatness when he stated: "Every philosopher has two philosophies – his and that of Spinoza." His writings, including his *Tracatus Theologico-Politicus, On the Correction of Understanding* and *Ethics*, have occupied philosophers ever since they were published. His philosophy greatly influenced Kant and Hegel, Marx and Nietzsche, Heine, Freud and Einstein.

It was Spinoza who stated: "By God, I mean a Being absolutely infinite, that is: substance consisting of infinite attributes, each one of which expresses eternal and infinite essence." "[A concept is not] an image which is seen by the retina or in the mind [but is a spiritual act] that the mind conceives as it is a thinking thing." "Truth is discrete, as is

untruth." "God and Nature are one."

Whatever exists in the world, he declared, is the reflection of existence as a whole. The world and everything in it – including man as a natural creature – is what actually exists. Furthermore, in the world we find the sole source for every ethical and political value and every norm. God Himself is identical, according to Spinoza, with the sum total of nature, and His laws are not written in the Torah but in the laws of nature.

Formulating and expanding these principles, Spinoza constructed a theory of knowledge, laid the foundations for Bible criticism, and established the framework for modern secularism and the political philosophy at its base. From him we learn, among others, that the democratic state, which is based on rational foundations, is the best of all states.

A descendant of Spanish Marranos who belonged to the Portuguese Jewish congregation in Amsterdam, Spinoza was not the representative of establishment Judaism. Not only, as every other great philosopher, was he alone, but his community excommunicated him and stated clearly that "no one is permitted ... to read any work he did or wrote." Nevertheless Spinoza is flesh of the flesh and blood of the blood of Judaism, his works rooted in Jewish history and Jewish tradition in the broadest sense (Hegel regarded his philosophy as "the most superior monotheism in the plane of thought"), and one can say that he was one of the greatest individuals to challenge Judaism. As Heine wrote: "The spirit of the Hebrew prophets hovers over this descendant of theirs," and that is why he occupies a place of honor in the contributions of the Jewish people to mankind's spiritual treasures.

The Jewish Academy

The secular liberal revolution in Europe, which Spinoza aided in initiating and carrying out, to a certain extent brought down the walls of the ghetto. The spirit of modernity which began to blow throughout Europe from the mid-18th century on also blew into the Jewish quarters and returned from them with renewed vigor. The changes it wrought were not simple – not in nature, not in kind, and not in the reciprocal relationships between them. Some of these changes ironically would lead to "scientific" anti-Semitism and to the state-sponsored hatred of Jews that fed the gas chambers and crematoria of Auschwitz. Some brought about a rebirth of the Jewish contribution to world culture in almost every realm of human endeavor.

In different guises, in varying circumstances, and having to pay a variable price for it, Jews entered Europe's universities and research institutions, attaining positions in the first rank of scholars and researchers, formulating new laws in science and medicine, founding academies and establishing new schools of thought, new social and economic theories, and making their own ineradicable mark on literature, the plastic arts and music, while their contributions were in no proportion to their size in numbers.

Not all acted as proud representatives of their nation. There were those who owed at least part of their success to the fact that they had cut themselves off from Judaism. Some were first, second or third generation converts, and there were those who simply denied their Judaism. In this context, perhaps it is relevant to mention the words of Benjamin Disraeli, baptized as a child and later prime minister of Great Britain. "When your ancestors were swine herders in the primeval forest," he said to a member of Parliament who

Maurycy Gottlieb (1836-1879) was one of the talented Jewish painters who sprang up in the small towns of 19th century Eastern Europe. During his short lifetime, he chose to paint mainly Jewish subjects, among them his famous "Jews Praying on the Day of Atonement" which includes the portrait of a young girl (above) through which he expressed his great sensitivity and remarkable insight.

mocked him for his Jewish roots, "my ancestors were priests in Solomon's Temple in Jerusalem."

The priests in Solomon's Temple or the farmers on the slopes of the Judean hills or the fishermen on the Sea of Galilee were also the ancestors of many of the shapers of the twentieth century. Three of these faithfully portray the essence of the story.

The most prominent, perhaps, was the theoretical physicist Albert Einstein (1879-1955). Born in Ulm, Germany, he left Germany for Italy and Switzerland, graduated from the Polytechnical Institute in Zurich, worked in the Swiss Patent Office, and in 1905 published three revolutionary theses: on the Brownian motion, on the photoelectric effect and on the special theory of relativity. The second thesis brought him the Nobel Prize in Physics (in 1921). The third made his name a household word and placed him amongst the ranks of the greatest physicists of all times. In this article, he laid down two hypotheses – that the laws of nature do not change in the eyes of observers who travel in various

The Sea of Galilee, focus of dreams and emotions. Theodor Herzl planned to establish an international institute for scientific research here.

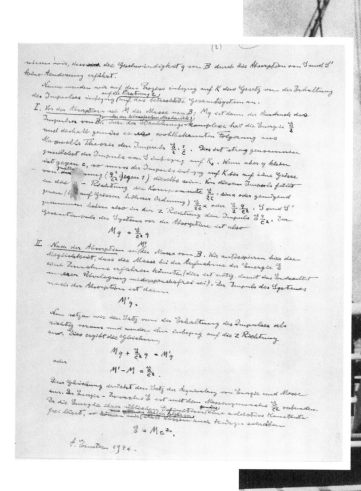

Albert Einstein, one of the greatest physicists of all time, the man who conceived the Theory of Relativity, went on to determine, among other things, the inter-changeability of energy and mass and by so doing made possible, for the first time, man's ability to employ atomic energy. In 1952 David Ben-Gurion offered him the Presidency of the State of Israel. Insert: Einstein's draft of one of his famous papers.

systems with relatively fixed movements, and that the speed of light is a fixed universal one – and from these he drew a number of dramatic conclusions. Among these was the famous equation, $E = mc^2$, expressing the possibility of transforming matter into energy and laying the theoretical foundation for the use of nuclear energy by man.

Later, in the midst of World War I, Einstein published his general theory of relativity, predicting that large masses of matter would produce a gravitational field which would "warp" the underlying four-dimensional space and would deflect light rays from their paths. The validation of this theory, during a solar eclipse in 1919, corroborated it and brought Einstein's popularity to a new high. He used his fame to condemn nationalism and to preach for an increase in international understanding, although he was not particularly successful in these efforts.

When Hitler rose to power in Germany, Einstein moved to the United States and called upon President Roosevelt to consider the possibility of manufacturing nuclear weapons, based on the equating of matter and energy. Thus the "Manhattan Project" was born, though its results were most displeasing to him, and he came out forcefully against the use of atomic weapons against Japan and preached for nuclear disarmament.

In his last years he attempted to develop a "unified field theory," an all-embracing theory which would include electro-magnetic and gravitational phenomena. In 1952, he rejected David Ben-Gurion's offer to become the second president of the State of Israel. Although honored by the idea, he claimed to be unsuitable for the task. It was like a continuation of one of his earlier statements that his belonging to the Jewish people had created in him "the striving for research for its own sake, the fanatic love for justice and the striving for personal independence."

Another brilliant thinker, who, like Einstein was one of the first members of the Board of Trustees of the Hebrew University of Jerusalem, Sigmund Freud (1856-1939), the founder of psychoanalysis, expressed himself similarly. In the introduction to the Hebrew translation of *Totem and Taboo*, he wrote: "Had I been asked, 'What remains to you of Judaism after you have left all forms of involvement with your people (i.e., Hebrew, religious faith, national ideals),' I would answer: 'very much, and probably the main part,' but I would not be able to express this idea in words."

He was born in Freiberg in Moravia, studied medicine in Vienna, was involved in research on the nervous system and specialized in psychiatry. Acquiring skill in this field, he decided that hysterical diseases can stem from a mental source – even without organic damage to the brain – and began to use hypnosis to disclose traumas from the past, thereby eradicating the neurotic symptoms. Then he went on to study the unconscious and repression, and showed their decisive role in psychopathological disturbances. In 1895, together with another Jewish scholar, Josef Breuer, he published *Studies in Hysteria*, considered to be the beginning of psychoanalysis and marking the shift of research into mental illness from the physiological to the psychological dimension. Following an innovative self-analysis, he published *The Interpretation of Dreams* in 1900, providing the major concepts of psychoanalytic theory. Here Freud reveals the infantile roots of the mind and the Oedipus complex, describes the laws determining our mental processes which occur in both the unconscious and conscious mind, and interprets various dream symbols to serve as a guide to the understanding of the unconscious.

Another book, *Three Essays on the Theory of Sex*, clearly and logically defined sexual deviation. Freud was also deeply involved in the psychoanalysis of children and in laying the groundwork for legal psychiatry and the modern treatment of criminals. His views on the relationship between emotional problems and physical illness gave birth to psychosomatic medicine. Freud was also the one who found that the mechanisms accounting for the behavior of the disturbed are also present in healthy people. It was he who forged the way to an in-depth understanding of psychosis. He was the founder of the dynamic method in psychiatry and of the psychotherapeutic era.

Furthermore, he investigated social and cultural phenomena from a psychological perspective, was most influential in the field of education and coined terms and concepts which have become part of our everyday life, even outside psychology. The sum total of his work marked a major watershed: the world before him was different from the one he left when he died in exile from Austria annexed to Nazi Germany.

Much the same may be said about literature before and after the great Jewish author, Franz Kafka (1883-1924). Born in Prague, he spent most of his life there, in that special blend of east and west, in Czech, German and Jewish cultures. Here, amidst terrible suffering, both physical and mental, he wrote his great works, including *The Metamorphosis, The Trial, The Castle* and *America*. Almost all describe a hero searching for identity, but confronting bureaucratic obstacles which are placed in his way, foil his plans and trap him. At the beginning of each story there is generally an event which is outside of everyday experience, while the continuation is realistic down to the smallest detail. Within the text and between the lines, the atmosphere of gloom and delusion deepens, along with uncertainty, despair

Sigmund Freud (1856-1939) – the Vienna-educated Jew who founded psycho-analysis, threw new light on the sexual factor in infancy and what he called the child's Oedipus complex in relation to its parents, and laid the foundations for modern ideas of education, psychology, religion, sociology and penal systems.

44

and nightmare, with the significance of the search for identity only hinted at. In any event, the inevitable failure of the hero, coupled with the obduracy and harshness of the legal system, combine to paint a picture characteristic of the author's writing (and, indeed, the word "Kafkaesque" has become a part of the universal vocabulary). Most commentators regard his as a supreme artistic expression of the mental distress and bewilderment of 20th century man, shifting from one extreme to the other – from the pessimistic view of nihilistic existentialism to faith in divine salvation.

"He was unable to pass the test in its entirety, he could not himself do the work of the authorities. The responsibility for the last mistake was because he had not utilized the remaining energy required for that act. His gaze rested at the top floor of the half-adjacent house. Like a sudden flash of light shining forth, suddenly the two sides of the window opened, and a man, thin and weak in the distance and at

"The Creation" – one of a series of lithographs by the well-known Israeli artist Mordechai Ardon.

Franz Kafka (1883-1924) (right; above, one of his letters) – the Jewish writer, born in Prague, whose impact on generations of writers and artists, in particular following World War II, was incalculable. The themes of confusion and despair, the quest for identity, alienation and the lack of answers or explanations faced by the always entrapped and doomed protagonist of his works, gave specific meaning to the term "Kafka-esque."

that height, wiggled outward at one fell swoop and spread out his arms even further than his body. Who was this? A friend? A good man? A man who had worked with him? A man who wished to help? Would he be the only one? Was this the entire community? Is there still help? Are there still claims and reasons which were forgotten and not stated? There are certainly such. But the logic is impeccable and unanswerable. But he is not standing before a man who wishes to live. Where is the judge, whom he has never seen? Where is the supreme court, which he had never reached? He raises up his hands and spreads all his fingers." These lines and others such as these made a profound impression on those writers who followed in his footsteps, especially after World War II and its monstrosities.

The work of these three – Einstein, Freud and Kafka – as great as it is, reflects but a small fraction of the contribution of Judaism to the civilization and culture of the modern era.

The full list embraces many in diverse fields, and includes, among others, the figure of the "dead man" (the "fiddler on the roof") of Marc Chagall, the "I-Thou" dialogue of Martin Buber, the "Tales of Hoffman" by Jacques Offenbach, and the magic violin of David Oistrakh. This list also includes the polio vaccine of Jonas Salk and of Albert Sabin, the mathematical genius of John Von Neuman, the films of Sergei Eisenstein and Ernst Lubisch, the chess virtuosity of Emmanuel Lasker and Mikhael Botvinik. Mention can also be made of statesmen such as Leon Blum and Pierre Mendes-France, who were French prime ministers, of Henry Morgenthau who served as the United States Secretary of the Treasury, and of Ezekiel Sasson who served in that capacity in Iraq. One can mention judges such as Louis Brandeis and generals such as John Monash, sociologists such as Claude Levi-Strauss and philosophers such as Herbert Marcuse, entertainers such as Woody Allen and newsmen such as Walter Lipmann. And this is but a minute fraction of the whole.

In any event, it would appear that it is worthwhile concluding this chapter with an instructive sample – the venerated place of Jews among the winners of the Nobel prize, this being the most illustrious award bestowed by the civilized world since 1901, an award given (in its own words) "to those people who have made the most important contribution for the good and the welfare of the human race." Here are the names of the Jewish Laureates, according to the six categories.

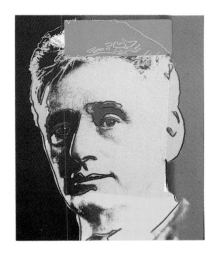

Louis Dembitz Brandeis (as seen by Andy Warhol) – who fought the large corporate interests in America on behalf of the "small man" and thus became known as "the people's attorney". In 1916, he became a Supreme Court justice and, at the same time, a confidant of President Woodrow Wilson.

Physiology and Medicine:

Paul Ehrlich (a pioneer in immunology and chemotherapy) and Elie Metchnikoff – 1908; Robert Barany – 1911; Otto Meyerhof – 1922; Karl Landsteiner (the discoverer of the different blood types) – 1930; Otto Warburg – 1931; Otto Loewi – 1936; Joseph Erlanger and Herbert Spencer Gasser – 1944; Ernst Boris Chain (for his part in the discovery of penicillin) – 1945; Hermann Joseph Muller – 1946; Tadeus Reichstein – 1950; Selman Abraham Waksman (the discoverer of streptomycin and neomycin and the one who coined the phrase, "antibiotic substances") – 1952; Hans Krebs and Fritz Albert Lipmann – 1953; Joshua Lederberg – 1958; Arthur Kornberg – 1959; Konrad Bloch – 1964; Francois Jacob and Andre Lwow – 1965; George Wald – 1967; Marshall W. Nirenberg (one of the decipherers of the

"Transformation and Fusion" by the celebrated Israeli artist, Yaakov Agam.

genetic code) – 1968; Salvador Luria – 1969; Julius Axelrod and Sir Bernard Katz – 1970; Gerald Maurice Edelman – 1972; David Baltimore and Howard Temin – 1975; Baruch S. Blumberg – 1976; Rosalyn S. Yalow and Daniel Nathans (a pioneer in genetic engineering) – 1978; Baruj Benacerraf – 1980; Cesar Milstein – 1984; Joseph Goldstein – 1985; Rita Levi-Montalcini and Stanley Cohen – 1986.

Chemistry:

Adolph Von Baeyer – 1905; Henri Moissan – 1906; Otto

Wallach – 1910; Richard Willstaetter (the discoverer of the structure of many natural substances) – 1915; Fritz Haber – 1918; George Charles de Hevesy – 1943; Melvin Calvin (the discoverer of the photosynthesis mechanism) – 1961; Max Ferdinand Perutz – 1962; William Howard Stein – 1972; Paul Borg and Walter Gilbert – 1980; Roald Hoffman – 1981; Aaron Klug – 1982; Sidney Altman – 1989.

Physics:
Albert Abraham Michelson – 1907; Gabriel Lippmann – 1908; Albert Einstein – 1921; Niels Bohr – 1922; James Franck – 1925; Gustav Hertz – 1925; Otto Stern – 1943; Isidor Isaac Rabi – 1944; Felix Bloch – 1952; Max Born – 1954; Emilio Segre – 1959; Donald A. Glaser – 1960; Robert Hofstadter – 1961; Lev Davidovich Landau – 1962; Richard Phillips Feynman and Julian Schwinger (the discoverers of the principles of quantum electrodynamics) – 1965; Hans Albrecht Bethe – 1967; Murray Gell-Mann – 1969; Dennis Gabor (a pioneer in holography) – 1971; Brian D. Josephson – 1973; Ben Mottelson – 1975; Burton Richter – 1976; Pyotr Kapitsa and Arno Penzias – 1978; Steven Weinberg and Sheldon L. Glashow – 1979; Leon Lederman, Jack Schwartz and Jack Steinberger – 1988; Jerome Friedman – 1990.

Shmuel Yosef Agnon (1888-1970), one of the central figures in Hebrew Literature, Nobel Laureate 1966.

Literature:
Paul Johann Ludwig Heyse – 1910; Henri Bergson – 1927; Boris Pasternak – 1958; Shmuel Yosef Agnon and Nelly Sachs – 1966; Saul Bellow – 1976; Isaac Bashevis-Singer – 1978; Elias Canetti – 1981; Nadine Gordimer – 1991.

Economics:
(the prize has been awarded since 1969):
Paul Anthony Samuelson – 1970; Simon Kuznetz – 1971; Jenneth Joseph Arrow – 1972; Leonid Kantorovich – 1975; Milton Friedman – 1976; Robert Morton Solow – 1987; Harry Markowitz and Morton Miller – 1990.

Peace:
Tobias M.C. Asser and Alfred Fried – 1911; Rene Cassin (for his contribution in drafting the International Declaration of Human Rights) – 1968; Henry Kissinger – 1973; Menachem Begin – 1978; Elie Wiesel – 1986.

Ninety years ago, in 1902, Theodor Herzl, founder of the Zionist movement, wrote a utopian novel named *Altneuland*, in which he sketched a profile of the Jewish state as he envisioned it. Among its important institutions was "the Jewish Academy." "When this institution was established," Herzl wrote, "its first members were selected from among different cultures and different languages, and their common humanity served to unite them." Herzl as its president made the following declaration: "Beauty and wisdom never disappear from the world. And even if those who propagate these die ... it is our duty to attempt to increase beauty and wisdom in the world until our last moments, because we are the world. We come from it and return to it."

And this is the first regulation that Herzl gave this institution: "It is the task of the Jewish Academy to ensure the rights of individuals who act on behalf of humanity." Herzl knew what he was talking about. Truth to tell, all he was doing was repeating two verses of the Bible: "I will make you a light unto the nations" and "Would that all the people of the Lord were prophets."

Eretz Israel Land of the Jewish People

About-to-ripen corn fields on the slopes of the Hebron hills (above) have been a feature of the landscape in these parts for thousands of years. (left) A Zodiac wheel from the mosaic floor of the 6th century B.C.E. synagogue found in Beit Alpha in 1929. Eretz Israel – at its center Jerusalem – as seen by a Christian pilgrim coming by sea and carved into a fifth century mosaic map discovered in 1884 in Madeba, Jordan. Eretz Israel is filled with reminders of antiquity. Opposite page: a clay figure from the Pottery – Neolithic culture, found in Munhata, the Jordan Valley (above); (below right): a scythe handle from the Natufian period, with a carved animal head, found in the Carmel caves; a stylized mace-head from the Judean desert, found among nearly 500 implements of the Chalcolithic period (below, left).

That "**Eretz Israel** (the Land of Israel) is the birthplace of the Jewish people" was stated at the beginning of the Declaration of Independence of the State of Israel and quoted at the beginning of the previous chapter. But by the same token, it can be said that it was the Jewish people who created Eretz Israel – as a concept and as a self-standing entity.

This stretch of land, which lies along the eastern shore of the Mediterranean, obviously existed before the appearance of man on earth. Indeed, there are places in the country – including Gesher B'not Yaakov, Tel Ubeidiya, Nahal Amud, the caves of the Carmel and Jericho – in which traces can be found of prehistoric societies. Already in the third millennium B.C.E. the Egyptian kings coveted it, referring to it as the land of the sand dwellers. At that time, the Canaanites already inhabited the country. And yet, Eretz Israel as a clear geopolitical entity, not as a chance collection of communities and settlements nor as an insignificant piece of land in an ancient empire, only became such when it turned into the land of one people – the Jewish people.

And that was also to be the case in later eras. Whenever the Jews were not sovereign in the land, there were those who made sure to obscure its unique identity, to carve it up or to annex it. The Persians included it in the large satrapy of Trans-Euphrates. The Romans partitioned it into individual provinces. The Muslims, who invaded it in the 7th C.E. from the Arabian peninsula, regarded it as part of their northern

ישראל במדבר בשנים

district (A-sham), namely Syria. The Ottomans divided it between their Damascus and Sidon provinces. Only the Jews – whether in Eretz Israel or in the Diaspora – remembered and perpetuated it as a single country. They did so in their minds and hearts, in their prayers and traditions, and in the books they took with them wherever they went – most especially the Bible.

The Book of Books is, among others, the history of Eretz Israel (Palestine) as the land of Israel. Almost from the start we find verses in which God makes a promise to Abraham, forefather of the Jewish people, in the following words: "Raise up your eyes and see from the place where you are, northward and southward and eastward and westward, for all the land which you see I will give to you and your seed for all eternity ... Unto your seed have I given this land, from the river of Egypt until the great river, the river Euphrates." It was to this land that the Children of Israel returned after fleeing Egypt, at the beginning of the 13th century B.C.E. At first they remained in the desert for forty years, but they had already learned about the promised land. In the Paran desert Moses heard the voice of God: "Send you forth men to spy out the Land of Canaan which I am giving to the Children of Israel." Thereupon Moses chose twelve leaders of the tribes and ordered them to "go up in the south and ascend the mountain. And see the land ... whether it is good or bad ... whether it is fat or lean, whether it contains trees or not. Gird yourselves and take of the fruit of the land." The spies returned after forty days, two of them bearing a pole on which they carried a gigantic cluster of grapes they had picked, and "pomegranates and figs," and they had this to say: "We came to the land ... and indeed it flows with milk and honey, and these are its fruits." As to the rest of their report, it was not unanimous. Ten of the spies were negative, claiming that "it is a land which consumes its inhabitants," and one which could not be conquered easily, while the two others, Joshua bin-Nun and Caleb ben Jephuneh, stated categorically: "The land is exceedingly good .. it is a land flowing with milk and honey." It was because of their devotion to the land that these two, and only they out of all of those who had left Egypt, would be privileged to "see the land which I swore to their fathers." Even Moses, the greatest prophet of all times and the leader of the nation, was not accorded this. As the Tribes

wandered about in the desert, Moses knitted these former slaves into one nation and saw to its moral instruction. He did not forget to tell them that "the Lord your God is bringing you into is a good land, a land of brooks of water, of fountains and depths that spring out of valleys and hills, a land of wheat and barley and vines and fig trees and pomegranates, a land of olive oil and honey, a land wherein you will eat bread without want, you will not lack anything in it; a land whose stones are iron, and out of whose hills you may dig brass." But Moses' fate was to see the land only from afar, not enter it. As God's last favor to him, he was permitted to ascend "from the plains of Moab to Mount

Nebo at the top of the hill facing Jericho," and to see, before his death, the spectacular view from there: "And the Lord showed him all the land of Gilead, to Dan, and all Naphtali, and the land of Ephraim, and Menasseh, and all the land of Judah, to the utmost sea, and the south, and the plain of the valley of Jericho, the city of palm trees, to Zoar." And once again the divine promise was proclaimed: "This is the land which I swore to Abraham to Isaac and to Jacob, saying 'to your seed I will give it.' "

The Mountain Shall be yours

From here on unfolds the history of the taking-over by the Jewish people of its land, within those borders that Moses saw as he stood at the peak of Mount Nebo. Naturally, this is a story of battles, of struggle against the local people who were not prepared to leave, against invaders by land and sea who coveted this fertile territory and against sectarian tendencies that threatened the Jewish people's national sovereignty. One must remember in this context that the Jews entered the land tribe by tribe, dividing it among themselves. Along those lines, it took a long time for them to realize the urgent need for unification and the benefit to be derived therefrom.

Many of the Jewish settlements were concentrated primarily in the hilly areas of the land, which were densely forested and uninhabited. Clear evidence of this is to be found in the Book of Joshua: "And Joshua spoke to the House of

The nation that conquered the Land under Joshua bin-Nun was organized into tribes, each receiving its own territory as detailed in the Book of Joshua. Rabbi Eliahu ben Shlomo Zalman, the "Vilna Gaon" (1790-1777), drew a map depicting this distribution – as in the Bible.

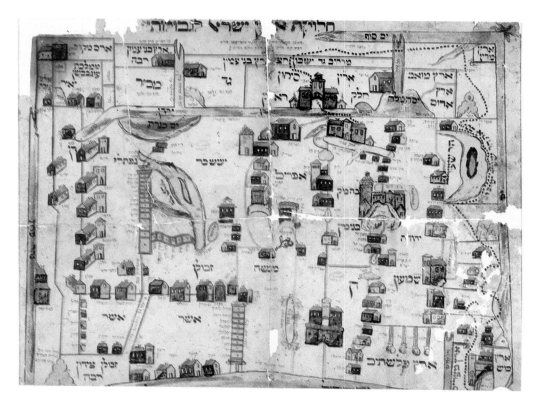

In Tel Dan, at the foot of Mount Hermon, among other finds, archeologists excavated 14th century B.C.E. Mycenaen utensils, (in the forefront) clear evidence of trade between Greek tribes and those of Eretz Israel. Background: collection of ancient pottery found in Jerusalem.

Joseph, to Ephraim and to Menasseh, saying, 'You are a great people, and have great power; you shall not have only one lot as your portion. The mountain shall be yours, for it is a forest, and you shall cut it down. And you shall possess it to the furthest limits.'' Once the people had taken over the land and begun to clear away the forests, they underwent a transformation; from a semi-nomadic group supporting itself by raising cattle, the Jews became a nation of farmers and of village and town dwellers. Many archaeological findings tell us about this process, aided, among others, by two important advances: the introduction of iron implements (which were used widely throughout the ancient Middle East from the time of the collapse of the Hittite kingdom), and the lining of wells with plaster so the people could store water systematically, thereby reducing their dependence on springs.

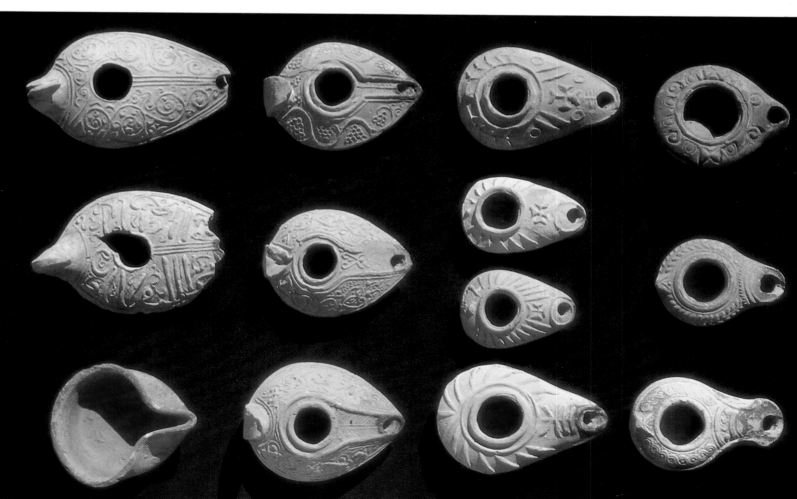

In any event, this was the first time in the history of Eretz Israel that there were settlements everywhere in the country, both in the valleys and in the hilly regions, and conditions were created for the nation's territorial and political unification. Moreover, the difficulties involved in this development contributed to the growth of an original, independent life style and culture able to preserve the spiritual values which this people had brought with it from the desert. It was on these advances that first Saul's kingdom (1025 – 1006 B.C.E.) was established, and then the kingdoms of David and Solomon (1006 – 928 B.C.E.).

During the reigns of David and Solomon, the Jewish rule extended over a sizable area: "On this side of the river, from Tipsah to Gaza" – from the Euphrates in the Syrian desert almost up to the Nile river. Within these boundaries, we are told: "Judah and Israel lived securely, each man under his vine and his fig tree, from Dan to Beersheba all the days of Solomon."

It was David who made use of the circumstances, who transformed Israel into a major power in the western part of the Fertile Crescent, who expanded its borders, made Jerusalem its capital, and established the state's organizational structure, and Solomon who changed it from a poor country limited in its interaction with its neighbors to a thriving international center. It was during the time of Solomon that the Temple was built on Mount Moriah, a symbol of the nation's existence and unity. At the same time, Solomon also built "the wall of Jerusalem and Hatzor and Megiddo and Gezer ... and Bet Horon below, and Baalat, and Tadmor in the wilderness, in the land, and all the cities of store that Solomon had, and cities for his chariots." He also expanded trade and was responsible for Israel's impressive cultural and technological progress.

After Solomon's death, the kingdom of Israel was divided into two separate political entities, Israel in the north and Judea in the south. It was natural that each was weaker than the unified kingdom had been, and indeed the borders soon eroded. Yet, in the mid-8th century B.C.E., the two kingdoms built up their forces and attained a sort of hegemony in the region. Jeroboam ben Joash, the king of Israel, "returned the borders of Israel from the entrance of Hamat to the Arava sea" (i.e., from the Lebanese Bek'a valley to the Dead Sea), while Uzziah, the king of Judea,

Opposite: Eretz Israel – Paradise of Archeology.

14-13th century B.C.E golden jewelry.

3rd century golden Jewelry.

Canaanite cult stand, late 10th century B.C.E

4th century Menorah stone relief.

Fragment of the pedestal of a 10th century ritual object.

6th century mosaic pavement.

9-10th century Hebrew inscription on mosaic pavement.

Below: a collection of 8th-12th centuries Islamic clay lamps, found in Jerusalem.

"built Eilat and restored it to Judea." We are also told that this king acquired a sea port: "He built cities in Ashdod and among the Philistines." Similarly, "Uzziah built strongholds in Jerusalem ... and fortified them. And he built strongholds in the desert and dug many wells, because he had much cattle, and in the valleys and plains, with farmers and vintners in the mountains and Carmel, for he loved land."

It was in this era that the great prophets whose words reverberate in the Bible were active. These were the days of Hosea and Amos, whose prophecies were directed to their Jewish brethren in both the kingdoms. Amos, born in Tekoa, Judea, went to Beth-El, in the kingdom of Israel, to cry out against "the three sins of Judea" and "the three sins of Israel." Similarly, Hosea cried: "What shall I do to Ephraim, what shall I do to Judah."

Amos ends his prophecy with a vision which is no less than a song of praise to the Holy Land: "Behold, days shall come when the one who plows shall overtake the reaper and the one who treads the grapes shall overtake the one who

"...Therefore the name of the city is Beer-Sheba unto this day." Modern Beer-Sheba, (above), one of Israel's largest cities, arose near Tel Beer-Sheba, thought to be the original settlement where this Hellenistic colored glass head insert was found.

carries the seed, and the mountains shall drip wine and the hills shall melt. And I shall return My captive people Israel and they shall rebuild ruined cities and dwell in them. They shall plant vineyards and drink their wine, and make gardens and eat their fruits. And I shall plant them on their land and they shall never again be uprooted from their land which I gave them." But this prophecy is preceded by a harsher one: "The eyes of the Lord your God are against the sinful kingdom, 'and I will destroy it from off the face of the earth, but I will not wipe out the House of Jacob,' says the Lord ... 'and I will shake the House of Israel among all the nations, as the grain is sifted in a sieve.' "

And this vision came to pass. In the year 722 B.C.E., "in the ninth year of Hosea, the king of Assyria captured Samaria and exiled its Jews to Assyria, and placed them in Halah and in Habor by the river of Gozan, and in the cities of the Medes." All the names of the areas mentioned have disappeared, and those exiled to them, the members of the

Ten Tribes, were lost, and now, according to Talmudic legend, live "inside the river Sambatyon." The embers, however, still flickered in Judea, which managed, though with great difficulty, to resist the Assyrians and to check their progress.

But the fate of this kingdom, too, was sealed. Though it recovered some of its grandeur during the days of Josiah (628-609 B.C.E.), when its borders also encompassed "the cities of Menasseh and Ephraim and Simeon up to Naphtali," eventually it fell before the Babylonian onslaught. In 589 B.C.E., Nebuchadnezzar, King of Babylon, embarked on a punitive mission against the tiny kingdom of Judea, leaving his imprint not only in the pages of the Bible, but also in the pottery shards which were discovered in Tel Lachish in 1935. In these one reads, "By the beacons of Lachish we remained on guard, in accordance with all the signs which the Lord gave that we would not see Azeka." And Jeremiah, the prophet of the destruction of the First Temple, would say regarding this: "The army of the king of Babylon waged battle against Jerusalem and against all the cities of Judea which remained, against Lachish and against Azeka, for these stayed in Judea as fortified cities."

A short time later, "in the fifth month on the seventh of the month, it being the nineteenth year of the reign of King Nebuchadnezzar the king of Babylon, there came Nebuzaradan, captain of the guard, who served the king of Babylon, into Jerusalem, and burned the house of the Lord and the king's house, and all the houses of Jerusalem and all the walls of Jerusalem they shattered ... and the rest of the people ... and the rest of the masses Nebuzaradan, the captain of the guard, exiled." And thus, in the year 586 B.C.E., the end came to the First Temple era, and the majority of Jews were torn away from their homes and driven into exile.

A measure of their grief and shock is reflected in one of the loveliest of the Psalms: "By the rivers of Babylon/ There we sat and cried/ As we remembered Zion./ We hanged our harps on the willows in its midst./ For there they that carried us away captive required of us a song;/ And they that despoiled us required us to rejoice, saying,/ Sing us one of the songs of Zion./ How shall we sing the Lord's song in a strange land?"

But the hope of returning to Eretz Israel never left those who mourned from afar. Despite their troubles and tribulations

and despair, there arose a prophet who, in addition to engaging in national soul-searching "within the exile by the river Kebar," proclaimed the vision of the dry bones: "Thus says the Lord God unto these bones: 'Behold, I will cause breath to enter into you, and you shall live' ... So I prophesied as I was commanded. And as I prophesied, there was a noise, and behold a shaking, and the bones came together, bone to its bone. And when I looked, lo, the sinews and the flesh came up upon them, and the skin covered them above, but there was no breath in them ... and the breath came into them, and they lived, and stood up upon their feet, an exceeding great army. Then He said to me, 'Son of man, these bones are the whole house of Israel. "Behold," they say, "Our bones are dried, and our hope is lost: we are cut off for our parts" ... Behold, my people, I shall open your graves, and cause you to come up out of your graves, and bring you into Eretz Israel ... and shall put My spirit in you, and you shall live, and I shall place you in your own land.' "

The Second Temple

In 539 B.C.E. Cyrus, king of Persia, conquered Babylon, "And he sent forth a proclamation throughout his kingdom as

"I will cause you to come up out of your graves and bring you into the Land of Israel." One of the strongest expressions of Jewish yearning for redemption is Ezekiel's vision of the dry bones, recreated in frescos in the third century C.E. Dura Europos synagogue on the Euphrates.

well as in writing, saying: ... 'Who is there among you of all his people that his God will be with him and will ascend to Jerusalem which is in Judea and will build the house of the Lord God of Israel, who is God, in Jerusalem.' " Thus began the period known in Jewish history and the history of Eretz Israel as the Second Temple era, and it was also the first time that the term "the return to Zion" was ever used.

In the first wave 42,360 people returned, under the leadership of Zerubabel ben Shealtiel, of the House of David, who bore the title "Governor of Judea," and of Joshua ben Jehozadak the priest. They settled in Jerusalem and its vicinity – from Bet El in the north to Bet Zur in the south, and from Jericho in the east to the slopes of the Judean hills in the west. The land to which they had returned was barren and waste, "and he who earned wages earned them to put them in a bag of holes." On all sides they were surrounded by hostile nations, among them "those who tormented Judea and Benjamin" and "the people of the land." The exaltation of returning to their homeland was soon replaced by the troubled feeling that this was "a day of small things," in the words of the prophet Zechariah. The building of the Temple took years, and was only completed in 515 B.C.E.

But the foundations were laid soon after the Return to Zion, and subsequent layers were laid on these foundations in the mid-5th century B.C.E., following the ascent of Ezra and Nehemiah.

Ezra, a priest and scribe, was active in the spiritual and religious realm. Nehemiah ben Hacaliah, cupbearer to King Artaxerxes I, arrived in Eretz Israel in 445 B.C.E. as the governor of Judea. Before leaving exile, he had laid down a challenge to his brothers: "Let us go and build the wall of Jerusalem and we will no longer be a disgrace." When he acted to fulfill this mission, he established a norm that would be employed by the Jews in their land for generations to come: "And it came to pass from that time forth, that half of my servants engaged in the work, and the other half held the spears, the shields, and the bows, and the armor; and the rulers were behind all the house of Judah. They who built on the wall, and they who bore burdens, and those who carried, every one with one of his hands engaged in the work, and with the other hand held a weapon. And the builders, every one had his sword girded by his side, and so they built."

Until the 4th century B.C.E., Eretz Israel was under the influence of the eastern empires. Then, with the appearance of Alexander the Great of Macedonia on history's stage, the country, like its neighbors, came under the influence of western culture, at first that of Greece and then that of Rome. In 332 B.C.E. Alexander conquered Eretz Israel from the Persians. He died nine years later, and the battles between his heirs involved all of the tremendous empire which he had founded; the houses of Ptolemy and Seleucus fought unceasingly for domination of the eastern Mediterranean. But not until the beginning of the 2nd century B.C.E. did a clear-cut victor emerge, when Antiochus III, a Seleucid king, took control. He recognized the Jews as an "ethnos" (i.e., a nation) whose capital was Jerusalem, and he permitted them to run their own lives peacefully, in accordance with their faith. The Jews seemed, on the surface, content with this arrangement, but in their hearts burned the hope of the restoration of Israel's greatness in all its glory. "Gather together all the tribes of Jacob and let them inherit as in olden days./ Take pity on the nation called by Your name, Israel whom you named firstborn," wrote Ben Sira, who was considered, if anything, one of the moderates. A short time later, in 175 B.C.E., Antiochus IV (Epiphanes) occupied the throne of the Seleucid kingdom. Intent on speeding up the hellenization of his subjects as well as on checking the Ptolemaic Egyptian kingdom in the south, he abandoned the practices of his predecessors, and high-handedly intervened in the concerns of the Jews in Eretz Israel, attempting to transform Jerusalem into a Greek polis and paganize it.

In 167 B.C.E., in the wake of various developments in the region in general, Antiochus issued a series of decrees: the Jews were forbidden to practice their religion in Judea, Samaria and Galilee; and whoever transgressed this decree in any way, from circumcising a baby to observing the Sabbath, was put to death. Furthermore, the authorities forced the Jews to engage in idolatrous rituals and forbidden customs, and especially to eat pork. The Temple, profaned, was consecrated to the Olympian god Zeus. This signalled the launching of a campaign of religious persecution without precedent in Jewish history then, one directed solely against the Jews. Only the Jews, of all the inhabitants of the empire, suffered for their beliefs. It was natural that it was they who ultimately rebelled, and, as a result of that rebellion, were

The rebellion against Antiochus was headed by the Hasmoneans, three of whom were buried at Modi'in, tradition has it, between the stones above. Below: from a German manuscript, fighting between Hasmoneans and the Seleucids whose force included elephants.

ultimately transformed from a small sect into the strongest nation in the region.

The rebellion was led by a small family of priests, the Hasmoneans, who lived in the town of Modi'in. The patriarch of the clan, Mattathias, issued a bold proclamation: "Even if all the other nations in the empire of the king obey him and abandon their beliefs and follow his commandments, I and my sons and my brothers will follow in the covenant of our fathers. Heaven forbid that we abandon the Torah and the commandments." This declaration was accompanied by a violent demonstration against the royal decrees, following which Mattathias and his family left for the hills to became what today would be called a guerilla force. Converting the land itself into an ally, their intimate knowledge of every crag and crevice in the country made it easy for them to move speedily from place to place, to identify the enemy's weak points, to confuse its plans and to evade it. In a short time, the family and its followers had completely undermined the enemy's hold on all but Jerusalem and inflicted severe defeats on the Seleucid army. And Judah the Maccabee, the son of Mattathias and his heir, told his "troops" before they embarked on a major battle near Bet Horon:

"It is easy to have many fall before few, and there is no difference before God whether to send deliverance by many or few, for it is not the large forces which ensure victory in the battle, but might is from heaven. They come to fight us with great conceit and evil, to destroy us and our wives and our children, to humiliate us. We fight for our souls and our Torah. He will drive them from before us and you need not fear them."

Judah led his men from victory to victory. In 164 B.C.E. he even conquered Jerusalem, purified the Temple, restored its sacrificial service, and established for all time the festival of Chanukkah. But even if religious freedom had been restored, the struggle was far from over. The Seleucids returned and attempted to regain the city, but the Hasmoneans, under Judah, met the challenge.

Judah was to fall in battle. "If our end is near," he said in his last days, "we will die bravely for our brothers, nor will we leave after us any blemish to our honor." His brothers, Jonathan and Simeon, took over the leadership, one following the other. Jonathan became the high priest and ruler of the land (which was still subject to the Seleucids); Simeon was already able to proclaim Judea's independence in 142 B.C.E. Now, according to the Book of Maccabees, "the yoke of the nations was removed from Israel and the Jewish people began to write 'In the first year of Simeon the high priest and commander and leader of the Jews.' "

Meanwhile, the borders of Judea were stretched. The grip of the Hasmoneans on the coastal plain was strengthened and they began to push into Samaria and Galilee. This was accomplished primarily by Johanan Hyrcanus, the son of Simeon the Hasmonean, and his son Jonathan, known as Alexander Yannai, who had himself anointed king. The kingdom Alexander Yannai bequeathed to his wife, Salome Alexandra (Shlomzion), extended from the Negev to the northern Galilee and included the entire coastal plain between what is now known as El-Arish to Carmel.

The reign of Shlomzion (76-67 B.C.E.) might be called the golden age of the Hasmonean dynasty. The queen kept control of the royal court and made peace between the various factions of the nation and showed great sagacity in

The Festival of Hanukkah has been observed in Israel and the Diaspora, sometimes even at the risk of one's life.

Above: a porcelain Chanukkah lamp from the Ukraine.

Below: a copper Chanukkah lamp from Poland.

Insert: a Chanukkah lamp from India in the shape of a Magen David.

her dealings with foreign countries. Thus, for example, she devoted much energy to preventing an invasion by the Armenian king, Tigranes, from Syria into Eretz Israel.

The quarrel between her two sons, which broke out after her death, coincided with the growth of the power of the Roman Empire. In 63 B.C.E., the famous Roman general Pompey entered Jerusalem at the head of a large army and abolished Jewish independence. In the decades that followed, the house of Antipater – with Roman sanction – ruled the land, but throughout those years there was an undercurrent of ferment that eventually led, among others, to the destruction of the Second Temple.

This ferment would be fed by social upheaval, by revolt against the foreign rule, by heavy taxation, by restrictions in religious observance and by foreign elements. One product of this era would be the establishment of the **bet midrash**, an institution open to anyone seeking to study the Torah. It was probably modelled to a certain extent on the Hellenistic academy, but it eventually became a pillar of the Jewish people. Another product of this dissatisfaction was the Dead Sea sect (the Essenes), a group which had retreated to live in the desert and to purify itself, in the hope of advancing the Kingdom of Heaven on earth. And then, of course, there were the developments which were directly responsible for the attempt by the Zealots, at the end of the seventh decade C.E., to take up arms against the Roman yoke. That rebellion ended in total defeat and in the shedding of much blood. Vespasian, before he became emperor, and his son Titus after him, crushed the Jewish revolt without mercy. Their troops besieged Jerusalem and, in the summer of 70 C.E., conquered it. The Temple was totally destroyed, and along with it the entire city, its inhabitants taken prisoner and sold into slavery. On the arch erected in Rome to commemorate Titus' victory is an engraving of a victory parade, displaying the seven-branched **menorah**, to signify the bitter defeat suffered by the Jews. Three years afterwards, the Roman army took over Massada, the last bastion of the Zealots.

From many points of view, this was the beginning of the almost total exile of the Jewish people from its land. But the glowing ember of freedom refused to die out altogether. More than sixty years later, the great Torah scholar Rabbi Akiva, and Simeon ben Kosiba (Bar Kochba), a high-ranking

military general, headed yet another uprising, this time against the Roman Emperor Hadrian. At first, in the year 132 C.E., the uprising seemed to augur well for the future. Bar Kochba was proclaimed **nasi** – the governor. He liberated Jerusalem, restored the outer facade of the Temple, minted coins and even began a new cycle of counting the years dating from "the freedom of Israel." But he failed to withstand the massive power of Rome – and one of its greatest emperors. In the fourth year of the revolt, 135 C.E., it came to an end. Of that time, it was later written in the Talmud: "For seven years the nations of the world grew their grape crops on ground soaked with Jewish blood, and so needed no fertilizer." That was the extent of the slaughter. Furthermore, a period of appalling persecution now began, one referred to in Jewish literature as the **shmad** – i.e., forced conversion. Hadrian decided to obliterate the Jewish settlement in Judea and to erase the national identity of the Jews in the rest of Eretz Israel. Mediterranean ports were filled with Jewish refugees; the number of captives so great that the price of slaves throughout the Roman Empire dropped. Jerusalem was plowed under and on its ruins a new city, Aelia Capitolina, constructed. To further expunge any hint of Jewish presence in the land, Hadrian ordered that Judea be renamed Syria Palestina. It was officially no longer the land of the Jews.

Next Year in Jerusalem

But the Jewish people, however vanquished, beaten and exiled, refused to accept the decree. Some Jews, not many, remained scattered in different parts of Eretz Israel, and managed to support themselves, even continuing to maintain the Jewish national institutions. Even at the time of the siege of Jerusalem by Vespasian, Rabbi Johanan ben Zakkai had left the capital and established a **bet midrash** in Yavneh, where he reinstated the Sanhedrin, the supreme Jewish religious (i.e., legal) authority. Now the Sanhedrin moved to Galilee – to Usha, to Shefaram, to Bet She'arim, to Zippori and then to Tiberias – continuing with its basic tasks: codification of the Oral Law – with the Mishnah completed in about 200 C.E. and the Jerusalem Talmud about 200 years later – and the issuing of rulings on germane issues. For example, it forbade the export of grain, oil and wine from Eretz Israel, in order to ensure a food reserve in the country, and ruled that small animals (sheep and goats) were not to

The synagogue at Capernaum on the Sea of Galilee – where Jesus preached, met his disciples and performed many of the miracles attributed to him – continued to function as such until the fourth century C.E. An unusual cornice frieze (above) shows the Ark on wheels.

Bet She'arim became in the 2nd century a necropolis not only for the Jews of Eretz Israel, but also for Jews from the Diaspora. Catacombs from the 2nd-4th centuries C.E. were discovered there, mostly of the general public. Decorations of sarcophages (inset) include reliefs with Jewish motifs.

be raised in cultivated land due to the destruction they caused as they grazed.

The Sanhedrin was regarded by the Jews in the Diaspora as the spiritual center of the people. It was from it, for example, that orders were issued each month as to when the special festivals of that month were to be observed, based on the sighting of the new moon. At first, before the destruction of the Second Temple, Jews were informed about the date of the new moon by means of flares on the Mount of Olives in Jerusalem. Once the flare was seen in Sarteba, those waiting there lit their own flare, which, in turn, was seen by those in Agrippina (probably Kochav Ha-Yarden), who then lit their own beacon. The chain extended to Hauran and then – evidently with way stations of which we are unaware – the flare was eventually seen in Bet Baltin, on the Euphrates, and in Pumpedita. As stated in the Talmud: "He would ascend to the top of the hill and light the flare there. He would wave it to and fro, up and down, until he would see the entire Diaspora before him like a bonfire." Later the system was done away with, and messengers were sent out

The Jewish calendar associates the Exodus and birth of the nation with Eretz Israel's farming cycle, so Diaspora Jews celebrating Shavuot, the "Time of the Giving of the Law" (for which 19th century Polish synagogues were adorned with paper decorations) simultaneously celebrated distant harvests.

from the Sanhedrin, a practice continuing up to the 4th century C.E., when a permanent calendar was introduced so that all Jews would know the time of the festivals, but this, too, was based on Eretz Israel.

Thus, for example, the Jews throughout the Diaspora went on counting the **omer** – the days in the seven week period between the cutting down of an **omer** (a certain measure of volume) of barley in Eretz Israel on the second day of Passover and the harvesting of wheat just before the **Shavu'ot** (Feast of Weeks) festival. In the Hebrew month of **Tishrei**, they celebrated the Festival of the Ingathering of the Crops, for this was when crops were brought into the barns in Eretz Israel. And their prayers for dew and rain were based on the rainy season in the Judean hills and the coastal plain.

This adherence to the Eretz Israel calendar was one of the factors referred to in the statement made in Israel's Declaration of Independence: "After being exiled from their land, the people kept faith with it throughout their Dispersion

and never ceased to pray and hope for their return to it and for the restoration in it of their political freedom." Torah scholars throughout the Diaspora in all generations debated the laws of the sabbatical year in Eretz Israel, and earnestly discussed the other laws which apply only to Eretz Israel. The standard prayer which Jews have prayed three times a day for thousands of years includes the request: "May our eyes see Your return to Zion."

They began grace after meals with the Psalm, "A song of ascents. When the Lord returned the captivity of Zion we were as in a dream," and in the Song of Songs they read such verses as, "My beloved is to me as a cluster of camphire in the vineyards of Ein Gedi;" "For, lo, the winter is past, the rain is over and gone; the flowers appear on the earth; the time of the singing of birds is come, and the voice of the turtledove is heard in our land. The fig tree puts forth its green figs, and the vines with the tender grapes give a good smell;" "Come with me from Lebanon, my spouse, with me from Lebanon. Look from the top of Amana, from the top of Senir and Hermon;" "Your hair is as a flock of goats that appear from Gilead."

They broke a glass beneath the wedding canopy to remind them of the destruction of the Temple, and ended the Passover **seder** meal and the **Yom Kippur** prayers with the wish "Next year in Jerusalem." They never stopped trying to realize this hope in practice in accordance with the Talmudic dictum: "A person should always live in Eretz Israel, even in a city with a majority of non-Jews, rather than live outside Eretz Israel in a city with a majority of Jews, for whoever lives in Eretz Israel is as one who has a God whereas one who lives outside Eretz Israel is as one who does not have a God."

In general, going to **Eretz Israel**, especially to settle, was defined as **aliyah** – an ascent, commemorating the **aliyah le-regel** – the three-times yearly pilgrimages to Jerusalem. The term also stressed the value of this deed. The **aliyah le-regel**, in its more limited sense – "Three times in the year all your males shall appear before the Lord" – was abolished in practice when the Temple was destroyed. But there is considerable evidence that Jews continued, without a break, to visit Jerusalem as though nothing had changed. Some even designated a fourth time of the year for such visits: the ninth day of the Hebrew month of **Av**, the day on which the Temple was destroyed, and there were those among them who went on from Jerusalem to visit the other holy places. We know that the number of those making such pilgrimages markedly increased after the Muslims conquered Eretz Israel in the 7th century and opened its gates to Jews living in Islamic lands. "The Holy One, blessed be He," a **midrash** of that time tells us, "will place over them (i.e., the Arabs) a prophet according to His will, and he will conquer the land for them, and they will come and build the cities, and clear the roads, and plant gardens and orchards." Not exactly what happened, but it is a fact that the Jewish settlement in Jerusalem was reconstituted, a community established in Ramleh, and the center in Tiberias (which in the Fatimid era moved to Jerusalem) greatly strengthened under Muslim rule. The situation worsened at the end of the 11th century, following the Crusader conquest of the land. The Crusaders were preceded by grim accounts of the murder and pillage they had engaged in against the Jews in Germany and France; and Jews in Eretz Israel, especially in the Haifa fortress and in Jerusalem, joined forces with the Saracens in opposing them – and paid heavily for this. When the

A page from a 15th century Italian Ketuba – Jewish marriage contract. Jewish bridegrooms traditionally smash a glass underfoot in memory of the Temple and with the hope of redemption. The Passover Haggadah (opposite) also recalls the same themes.

In 1095 Pope Urban II called upon Christians to join in the deliverance of Jerusalem, especially the Holy Sepulcher, from the Infidels. For roughly the next 200 years, Crusaders battled Muslims in the Holy Land. Below, from a French manuscript, a picture of the fighting. Right: the Crusade fortress Kalaat Nimrud, near Mount Hermon.

Crusader kingdom was established in Jerusalem, all non-Christians were forbidden to live there. Even in 1129, Rabbi Abraham ben Yihye of Barcelona was still forced to write: "Ever since these wicked ones conquered the Temple area, they have not permitted Jews to enter it. Not a single Jew is to be found in Jerusalem in these days." That, in reality was the situation in all the cities of Eretz Israel, except for Tyre and Ashkelon. In any event, at the beginning of the 12th century there was a change in the way the Crusaders related to the local populace, including the Jews, who were permitted to return and settle in all the cities except for Jerusalem (which, nevertheless, could be visited) and to maintain their own communities and courts of justice.

One of the most poignant moves to Eretz Israel was that of Yehuda HaLevi. Rabbi Yehuda HaLevi was born in Spain in the late 11th century, and soon became the poet who most memorably expressed the Jews' longing for Zion. It was he who wrote, among others, "My heart is in the east and I am at the end of the west./ How shall I taste that which I eat and how can it please me?/ How shall I make good my vow and my oath/ For Zion is in the Edomite lands and I in the Arab./ It would be easy for me to forsake all the goodness of Spain/ For more precious to me is the sight of the dust of the destroyed Temple." In 1140 he decided to move to Eretz Israel. No one knows if he succeeded in this, but we are told in Jewish legend that he reached the Western Wall and there lamented: "Zion, do you not inquire for the wellbeing of your captives?/ Those seek your welfare and what is left of your flock/ ... When I weep for your humiliation I am like a jackal, but when I dream/ Of the homecoming of your captives/ I am like a harp for your songs./ You are the royal house and God's throne/ And how shall slaves sit on the thrones of your nobles?" And then, according to this legend which formed the basis for one of Heine's best-known poems, an angry Christian horseman trampled him to death.

Another noted immigrant to Eretz Israel was Rabbi Moses ben Nahman, known as Nahmanides, who arrived in Jerusalem in 1267 and found it in ruins, its entire population consisting of two thousand souls, "without a Jew among them," wrote Nahmanides to his son, "except for two brothers who are dyers and buy their dyes from the governor. On Sabbaths, a few more Jews assemble in their home, so that they have a **minyan**" (a quorum of ten). But Nahmanides also pointed out there was a ray of light at the end of the tunnel: the continuous arrival of Jewish pilgrims in Jerusalem. He arranged that Torah scrolls which had been smuggled to Shechem (Nablus) for safekeeping be returned to Jerusalem, and he worked to establish a synagogue there. There are those who claim that this synagogue stood exactly where the Nahmanides synagogue in the Old City of Jerusalem stands today. Nahmanides also stressed the Talmudic statement that "living in Eretz Israel is equivalent to all of the other commandments," and added: "Our land does not accept our enemies." [One of his students formulated this as follows: "Let no one think that the King Messiah will appear in an impure land, or err by thinking that he will even come to Eretz Israel among the non-Jews."]

In 1313, Rabbi Eshtori Ha-Parhi immigrated to Eretz Israel, settling in Bet Shean, where, nine years later, he published

Spanish-born Benjamin of Tudela, the most famous Jewish traveler of the Middle Ages, reported in the 12th century that only 1500 Jewish families lived in Eretz Israel. In his "Itinerary" (above) he described the Holy Places and Jerusalem in much detail.

his **Kaftor Va-Ferah**, a collection of laws dealing with Eretz Israel and based on the conditions actually prevailing in the land then. This is a major firsthand source of information about the settlements in the Middle Ages and helps us deal with various problems in the interpretation of the Bible and Talmud. More than 150 years later, Rabbi Isaac Sarfaty wrote to "the holy Jewish communities in Germany," that even though "a decree was issued that you cannot sail by sea ... the route through Turkey is a viable one, a completely dry road until Jerusalem."

And indeed the route through Turkey was shown to be suitable for immigration in the wake of two historic events: the expulsion of the Jews from Spain in 1492 and the Ottoman conquest of Eretz Israel in 1516. These events resulted in large-scale immigration to Jerusalem and, on even a larger scale, to Safed, which became the seat of an important spiritual center, based on the mystical thinking of the kabbalah.

The kabbalah, which began to develop among the masses of Spanish Jewry in the 13th century, was brought to Safed, the major city in Galilee, because it was believed that the book on which the kabbalah is based, the **Zohar**, was authored by Rabbi Simeon bar Yochai, who is buried in Meron, near Safed, and also because of an ancient tradition that has it that the Messiah will be revealed in Galilee. The greatest scholar of the **Zohar** was Rabbi Isaac Luria, the **Ari**, who also lived in Safed and who formulated the concept of **tzimtzum** ("contraction") – that the Godhead, which filled the entire universe, "contracted" within itself to permit the creation of the world. From this point, the **Ari** went on to develop concepts such as the exile of the divine presence "among the **klippot**" (the "husks" of impurity) and the desire for cosmic redemption; ideas and symbols that would later give birth to two important social movements, Sabbateanism and Hassidism.

In addition to the **Ari**, others were active in Safed at the time, among them Joseph Caro, the greatest authority on Jewish law and the author of **Shulchan Aruch**, the compilation of Jewish law. So too were there the kabbalists Moses Cordovero and Hayyim Vital, the poet Solomon Alkabetz (author of the poem **Lecha Dodi**) and the head of the community, Jacob Berab, who sought to reinstitute the Biblical rabbinic ordination.

The 16th century kabbalah movement found final form in the Galilean town of Safed where its founder Rabbi Isaac Luria ("Ha-Ari") settled. The influence of his poet-disciples was strongly felt in the prayer book (above). Published in Morocco in 1797.

Safed's Sephardic synagogues have been in use longer than any others in Eretz Israel; the "Ari" synagogue (opposite) dating to before the 15th century. Safed's charm has always attracted artists; Nahum Gutman (his water color "Pomegranates in Safad" (opposite, below) was one such artist.

The 18th century brought to Eretz Israel the Sabbateans, i.e., the disciples of the false messiah Shabbetai Tzvi (1626-1676), who hoped by their actions to bring forward the redemption and even awaited the return of Shabbetai Tzvi himself in Jerusalem. At the end of that century there was a wave of immigration of Hassidim, who settled in the four holy cities of Eretz Israel: Hebron, Jerusalem, Safed and Tiberias. Their number included Rabbi Nahman of Bratislav, a Ukrainian Hassidic rabbi who stayed for only a short time, though it was he who stated, "Wherever I travel, my destination is Eretz Israel." Later, at the beginning of the 19th century, Mitnagdim, disciples of Rabbi Elijah of Vilna and opponents of the Hassidic movement, began to arrive, settling mostly in Jerusalem.

We should also take note of the immigrants from Morocco and Algeria who sailed to Acre at the end of the 1830's, bound for Safed. Their ship was caught in a storm off Haifa and twelve of those on board were killed. The rest managed to make it ashore and wandered about in the country until they settled in Jaffa. There, they played a significant role in revitalizing the Jewish community of the city.

The National Home

In 1862, a book was published in Germany entitled, *Rome and Jerusalem*. Its author, Moses Hess, one of the heads of the international socialist movement, wrote in his introduction: "I have returned, after twenty years of alienation, and am among my people, a participant in their festivals, their joys and their mourning, in their remembrances and in their hopes." Afterwards, he declared: "With the liberation of the Eternal City on the banks of the Tiber, there will also begin the liberation of the Eternal City on Mount Moriah. With the renaissance of Italy there will begin the renaissance of Judea. The orphaned sons of Jerusalem will also be permitted to take their place in the great revival of nations." That same year *Derishat Tziyon (The Seeking of Zion)* was published by Rabbi Tzvi Kalischer, in which he wrote: "Why is it that the people of Italy and of other countries willingly sacrifice their lives for the land of their fathers, while we stand from afar, as a powerless man with no heart? Are we less than the nations, whose blood and property are as nothing when compared to their country and people?" Even earlier, in 1845, Rabbi Yehuda Hai Alkelai, a Sephardic rabbi

Ceaseless Jewish striving for redemption gave rise to various messianic movements. Best-known was that of Shabbetai Tzvi (1626-1676) who aroused the hopes of Jews everywhere, but eventually became a Muslim and died in exile. Above, Tzvi in Smyrna, from a 17th century book.

in Sarajevo, had written an essay explaining that: "We must build houses and dig wells and plant vines and olives ... Our brothers in the Diaspora will help those who immigrate from the Diaspora for we may assume that the first immigrants will be very poor." He himself settled in the Holy Land in 1874. Hess, Kalischer and Alkelai wrote as they did against the background of the reawakening of European nationalism which, coupled often with violent anti-Semitism, the perpetual poverty of the Jews and the longing for redemption that had pulsed in them for so long, would soon bring about a single revolution with two clear aims, a revolution to be referred to at the end of the 19th century as Zionism. On the one hand, the Jewish national movement would be formed to solve the problems of the Jewish people; on the other, new circumstances would be created in Eretz Israel to serve as the basis for solving these problems in the historical land of the Jews.

So circumstances began to be created in Jerusalem. If, at the beginning of the 19th century the Jewish community in that city was the smallest of the three principal Jewish communities in Eretz Israel, by 1840 it already numbered about 5,000 Jews (as opposed to 3,300 Christians and 4,650 Muslims). The area within the Old City walls soon became overcrowded and in 1856 the move outside the walls began. With the aid of overseas patrons, the Jews of Jerusalem built the first three neighborhoods outside the walls: Mishkenot Sha'ananim, Mahaneh Yisrael and Nahalat Shivah, so that by 1880 there were already 2,000 Jews living in nine neighborhoods of New Jerusalem.

Meanwhile, in 1870, the secretary general of the Alliance Israelite Universelle, Charles Netter, arrived in Eretz Israel and established a Jewish agricultural school, Mikveh Yisrael, near Jaffa, a first step in the re-entry of the Jews into the country's agriculture after close to 2,000 years. Over the following years, a group of Jerusalem Jews attempted to buy land in different regions of the country in order to establish an agricultural settlement. In 1878 they succeeded. They acquired land near the Yarkon river and set up Petah Tikva, "the mother of the settlements." In their first year of operation, they were able to grow wheat and produce bread. Then their troubles began. Floods, malaria, poor yields and internal dissension joined together to cause the settlers to temporarily abandon the area at the end of 1881. When they returned to it, a year or two later, the First Aliyah (immigration) wave was already in progress.

Its first members arrived in Eretz Israel from Yemen, having travelled through the desert, following a messianic upsurge that swept their community. At almost the same time, the mass migration of Jews from Russia began, following the pogroms of 1881-82, with a small percentage of these Jews immigrating to Eretz Israel. Those who did so included a group of students who called themselves the Bilu, this being an acronym of the Hebrew verse, "House of Jacob, let us go and advance." They settled in Mikveh Yisrael, afterwards moving to Rishon Le-Zion, an agricultural settlement established in 1882, and then to their own settlement, Gedera, founded in 1884. They were the first Jews to have settled on the land for ideological reasons, the ideology later to be called Zionism.

Almost at the same time as the founding of Rishon Le-Zion, two groups of immigrants from Romania founded Rosh Pina and Zichron Yaakov. These three settlements soon found themselves faced with serious financial problems. It was Baron Edmond de Rothschild (later known as "the father of the Yishuv" – i.e., the Jewish settlement in Eretz Israel, as well as "the renowned philanthropist") who stepped in to offer them generous assistance, aiding in particular the planting, among others, of vineyards for the production of wine.

In 1870, Charles Netter of the Alliance Israélite Universelle founded the Mikveh Israel Agricultural School. Theodor Herzl stayed in its first building (opposite), when, in 1898, he met with Kaiser Wilhelm II at the school gates. Insert, the first grape harvest, Rishon Lezion, the 1880s.

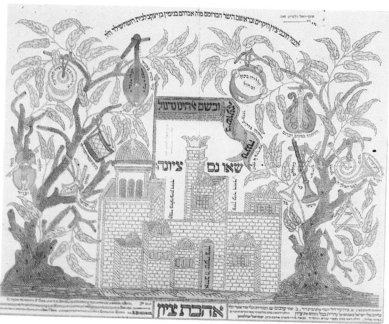

In 1883 a new settlement, Mazkeret Batya, was founded, and near it Nahalat Reuven was established (which would later be renamed Nes Tziyona). In 1884, Yesud Ha-Ma'aleh was established along the shores of the Huleh swamp. This was followed by Bat Shlomo, Rehovot, Mishmar Ha-Yarden, Hadera and Metulla. At the beginning of the 20th century, a few more settlements were founded in the Lower Galilee. By the time the First Aliyah wave had run its course, there were 23 agricultural settlements throughout the land, their population exceeding 5,000. But the beginnings were uniformly difficult. Malaria was the settlers' constant companion, their adaptation to the climate and to hard agricultural labor was acquired painfully, the ruling Ottoman government doing everything possible to undermine them and their financial circumstances precarious in the extreme. Some of the settlements were ultimately abandoned and there was ample reason for disappointment, despair and frustration. Still, the foundations had been laid.

Among those who helped in laying these foundations were the "Hovevei Zion," groups of Eastern European Jews who had begun to formulate what would become the ideology of modern Zionism, to collect money for the settlement effort, and also – here and there – to form groups which moved to Eretz Israel. Their leader was Dr. Leo Pinsker, the author of *Autoemancipation*, a pamphlet in which he declared the Jews in the Diaspora would always remain alien to their surroundings and he prescribed a single cure: "the creation of the Jewish nation, a nation living on its own land." Toward the end of the 19th century, the Hovevei Zion

מ י ת ן מ צ י ו ן י ש ו ע ת י ש ר א ל.

301

האדון

הכנים

בשובה ונחת תושעו, בהשקט ובבטחה תהיה גבורתכם.

The first Zionist Congresses took place in Basle, Switzerland, with delegates attending from all over the Jewish world. The Shekel (insert), was declared the unit of Zionist membership dues.

merged with a larger movement, which proudly hoisted the flag of Jewish nationalism. In 1895, following the Dreyfus case, a Viennese journalist, Theodore Herzl, wrote a 68 page treatise which he called *Der Judenstaat* – (The Jewish State), which was subtitled, "An attempt at a modern solution to the Jewish problem." This treatise was published a year later. The next year, Herzl convened the first Zionist Congress in Basel, Switzerland. The 204 delegates who arrived from all over Europe, Eretz Israel and the United States, declared themselves the national assembly of the Jewish people and approved the Basel Program: "Zionism strives to create for the Jewish people a home in Eretz Israel, secured by public law. To achieve this aim, the Congress determines the following means: 1) the settling of Eretz Israel by Jews who will work the soil, by craftsmen and by industrialists in a manner suitable to the aim; 2) the organizing and unifying of the entire Jewish people by means of appropriate institutions, both local and general, in accordance with the laws of each country; 3) the strengthening of the national Jewish feeling and of Jewish national recognition; 4) preparatory work toward obtaining the agreement of the different nations to the Zionist aim."
"In Basel I founded the Jewish state," wrote Herzl in his diary when the Congress was over, and added that "I do not know whether my vision will be realized within five or within fifty years." In reality, what was needed was somewhat more than half a century, a period of ups and downs, high points and low, and which included the Nazi Holocaust which wiped out more than a third of the Jewish people.
Zionism set out on its way – with a blue and white flag and

91

an anthem which spoke of "the two thousand year hope (**Ha-Tikvah**) to be a free nation in our land, the land of Zion, Jerusalem." Its emissaries began to spread its message throughout the Jewish world and to attempt the attainment of international recognition. But its actions were mainly concentrated in Eretz Israel itself. After the Zionist Movement was established, the Second Aliyah began, lasting from 1903-1914. It brought with it added impetus to the agricultural settlements and also, in the words of one of Zionism's historians, "a dream, a legend, great plans and Zionist utopianism."

The Second Aliyah also brought to the land about 20,000 – 30,000 people, including a young, vibrant nucleus which established the Eretz Israel labor movement and left a profound impression on the life style of the Yishuv (as the Jewish community in Eretz Israel was referred to until the establishment of the State of Israel). Those who came in this Aliyah were involved in the conquest of labor and the conquest of the land, and pioneered a series of new patterns and social vehicles. In one of these years, 1909, three major enterprises were established, without prior coordination. These were the first **kibbutz**, Deganiah; the

Kfar Tabor, established 1901 under Mount Tabor (as seen, below, by Yehoshua Brandstetter), was the cradle of "HaShomer" (insert opposite) which grew into the Haganah and I.D.F. The second wave of immigration, starting 1903, launched the now-flourishing kibbutz movement in the Jordan Valley (opposite).

first Jewish self-defense force, **Ha-Shomer**; and the first all-Jewish city, Tel Aviv. It was also the Second Aliyah that revived Hebrew as a spoken language, and during this era the educational system was expanded. There was also a renewal of immigration from Yemen. In short, it was the Second Aliyah which ensured that the First Aliyah and the infant Zionist movement would not be merely transitory episodes.

World War I brought a dramatic change to Eretz Israel. It marked the end of four hundred years of Ottoman rule in the Middle East, now brought under the patronage of the two European superpowers – Britain and France. During the war, the Zionist movement, under the leadership of Chaim Weizmann, had received the Balfour Declaration from the British government. Published on November 2, 1917, as the British forces drew nearer to Eretz Israel, it stated: "His Majesty's Government view with favour the establishment in Palestine of a national home for the Jewish people and will use their best endeavours to facilitate the achievement of this object."

Immediately afterwards, a shock wave, as it were, passed through the Jewish world. There were those who compared the Balfour Declaration to the proclamation issued by King Cyrus in 539 B.C.E.: "Whoever among you among his people, may his God be with him and may he ascend to Jerusalem." Many hoped that full redemption would now come about, almost automatically. But reality dampened their hopes. The Declaration would not suffice.

Each wave of subsequent immigration, or the Third, Fourth and Fifth Aliyahs, brought its own kind of individual, its own set of problems, achieved its own successes and conducted its own struggles. The investment of effort and resources now required for expansion of the Jewish settlement, for production of weapons and the creation of social structures, was immense. The 1930's and 1940's were to witness a defensive war by the Jewish settlement against Arab hostility and fierce differences of opinion within the Yishuv as to the proper path of the Zionist enterprise, as well as the heroic smuggling of Jews who did not accept British quotas on their entry into Eretz Israel and sought to reach it by "illegal" means.

Meanwhile, dark clouds loomed overhead as the Jews of Europe faced a terrible fate. In January 1933, Hitler became

The "Stockade and Tower" settlements (above by Ziona Tagger) expressed the Yishuv's response in 1936-1939 to Arab violence and Mandatory hostility: instant establishment of new settlements, consisting of little more than fences and a watch-tower. Below, Tel Aviv rising from the dunes, 1922, as seen by Reuven Rubin.

chancellor of Germany, and embarked on ventures which took the entire world into World War II and dragged the Jewish people into the gas chambers. The anti-Semitism which had been part of the very fabric of Europe for hundreds of years was now transformed, monstrously, into a major component of the actions and policies of one of Europe's most important states. What had begun as attacks against Jews and their property developed into the "Final Solution." Even while it was engaged in an aggressive war against a large coalition, in the midst of a satanic attempt to conquer all Europe, Nazi Germany also occupied itself with the methodical murder of millions of Jews in the areas it conquered, including in the ghettoes in which they were first brutally confined. Thousands of trains criss-crossed the continent, carrying the men, women and children of the "inferior race" to concentration camps where they were killed solely because they were Jews. The killing machine did not pause even in the last year of the war, when it was clear that Germany was headed for total defeat. Even then the furnaces continued to emit their dreadful smoke. Even then the Jewish people were murdered.

They were killed because they were despised, but also because the gates which should have been opened to offer refuge were barred to them – and they had no state of their own, which would offer them a haven in troubled times. This tragic lesson was not least of the factors that spurred the struggle of the Jews for political independence in Eretz Israel after World War II.

Now or Never

On November 29, 1947, the General Assembly of the United Nations, sitting at Lake Success, New York, decided on the termination of the British mandate in Eretz Israel and on the partition of the land into two sovereign states, one Jewish and one Arab. The Jewish state was to have an area of 14,000 sq. km. and did not include Jerusalem or the road to it or most of the Galilee. In two areas, in the southern Judean plain and in the Jezreel valley, its width was reduced to almost nothing. But the Jewish people in Eretz Israel and elsewhere accepted the proposal with enthusiasm. A few hours after the dancing in the streets had ended, Eretz Israel was in the throes of the War of Independence.

"That which was written in Lake Success in ink will be erased in Palestine in blood," said a head of the Arab Higher

Severe restrictions on the immigration of the Holocaust survivors (above), and the Jewish right to own land in Eretz Israel. (Opposite, right). The focus of a 1944 Jewish Federation of Labor May 1st poster is not class warfare but the White Paper (left). Crowds celebrate the November 29, 1947 decision – despite the State's projected size and the omission of Jerusalem, and Arab threats. Next day the War of Independence began.

Committee – and indeed blood began to flow, even though
the resolution was not erased. The Jews of Eretz Israel,
numbering only some 600,000 people, fielded an army
which, at its peak, accounted for 70,000 fighters, most of
them trained for years in the underground Jewish
self-defense Haganah or in the ranks of the British army in
World War II. A lesser number were members of the small
secret **Etzel** and **Lehi** forces, along with survivors of the
Holocaust and foreign volunteers. At first the Jews fought
only with light weapons collected from various sources, with
very limited ammunition. But what they lacked in weapons
they made up for in their spirit, in their readiness to sacrifice,
and in their feeling that "there is no choice."
The first months of the war were fought against the local
Arabs, against an "army" of volunteers from Arab states and
against the British authorities who aided them. This was
primarily a battle for roads, for cities with mixed Jewish-Arab
populations and for isolated settlements. By March 1948, the
situation almost reached crisis proportions: the Arab forces

Arab forces invaded Israel the day after the State was declared. They were only prevented from overrunning the country by the exemplary courage and devotion demonstrated by the Jewish defenders.

were on the verge of dividing the Jewish area into sections cut off from one another; the regular forces of the Arab states threatened to invade the country and intervene in the battles; and the British blockade of the shores of the country prevented the bringing in of people and equipment to aid the Jewish fighters. But the Jewish forces showed their mettle, opened the road to Jerusalem and defeated the "volunteer army." Following this, "Operation D" was put into effect, and a territorial continuity was created encompassing almost all the Jewish settlements, enabling the Jews to withstand the expected invasion of the Arab armies.

At the beginning of May, Jewish commanders estimated the chances of victory as 50-50, and preparations were made for declaring independence in mid-month in accordance with the UN resolution of November 29. The debate whether to take this step intensified, especially when the United States government sent signals regarding the need for postponement. In the midst of this debate, the famed French-Jewish statesman, Leon Blum, whose advice had been sought, stated: "Now or never." Immediately afterwards, David Ben-Gurion, leader of the Jewish community of Eretz Israel, tipped the balance and decided: "Now."

And so it happened that on Friday, May 14, 1948, representatives of the Yishuv met together in the small Tel Aviv museum and decided: "On the day of the termination of the British mandate over Eretz Israel and, by virtue of our natural and historic right and on the strength of the resolution

of the United Nations General Assembly, we hereby declare the establishment of a Jewish state in Eretz Israel, to be known as the State of Israel." The Declaration of Independence then added that "The State of Israel will be open for Jewish immigration and for the Ingathering of the Exiles; it will foster the development of the country for the benefit of all its inhabitants; it will be based on freedom, justice and peace as envisioned by the prophets of Israel; it will ensure complete equality of social and political rights to all its inhabitants irrespective of religion, race or sex; it will guarantee freedom of religion, conscience, language, education and culture; it will safeguard the Holy Places of all religions; and it will be faithful to the principles of the Charter of the United Nations ...

"We appeal to the Jewish people throughout the diaspora to rally round the Jews of Eretz Israel in the tasks of immigration and upbuilding and to stand by them in the great struggle for the realization of the age-old dream – the redemption of Israel."

That night, the armies of Egypt, Transjordan, Syria, Lebanon and Iraq, invaded the new-born State in accordance with a comprehensive plan "to destroy the Zionist entity" within ten days. The second stage of the War of Independence had begun. The first wave of battle lasted until June 11, 1948, during which most of the invading force had been checked. The battle continued for ten days in July, and afterwards from October until the beginning of January 1949. Only then did Egypt declare that it was willing to sign a cease-fire, and was followed by Transjordan, Syria and Lebanon.

The war ended. Israel now contained 20,700 sq. km.. from Metulla in the north to Eilat in the south – including considerable tracts of land not allocated to it in the partition resolution, including western Jerusalem and the corridor leading to it, the Galilee and Negev. The borders were determined by adding to the map of Jewish settlement activity those areas won by the new State's army in its battles for survival. And in the military cemeteries lay more than 6,000 soldiers, one percent of the Jewish population of Eretz Israel having paid with their lives for the renewal of Jewish sovereignty after close to two millennia.

One of the first laws promulgated by the State of Israel was the Law of the Return. Its first paragraph states: "Every Jew has the right to come to this country as an **oleh**," which a footnote defines as "a Jew immigrating to Israel for settlement." This established the fact that there could never again be a situation such as that which preceded the Holocaust and lasted through it. No Jew will ever have to face sealed gates in Eretz Israel.

This law was passed in the midst of the mass immigration wave which accompanied the establishment of the State. In its first four years, more than 700,000 new immigrants arrived in Israel, more people than had lived in Eretz Israel at the time of the declaration of the State. Approximately half hailed from the Islamic lands and half from Europe. A few years later there was another immense wave, with an additional 200,000 people. Between them, these two waves, more than any other factor, changed the face and destiny of the Jewish state.

It was natural that the assimilation of so huge a number into the new state would result in major problems – from a shortage of food which required rationing and the massive intervention of the government in the economy to ensure housing for all, to a need to find work and build a proper physical infrastructure. Some of these problems would leave their imprint on the State, and on Israeli society, for many years.

At the same time, with the help of the Jewish people throughout the world, the State of Israel was able to cope with its central challenges. A striking example was in the area of settlement: In the 65 years which preceded the Declaration of Independence, 277 Jewish settlements were established, while in the five years after it another 284 were

founded. These settlements, and those which came after them, were situated along the Lebanese border, in western Galilee, in the area between the Huleh and the Sea of Galilee, along the Jordanian border from the Bet Shean valley to the southern Jezreel valley and to western Samaria, eastern Sharon and the Jerusalem Corridor. At the same time, the entire area between Tel Aviv and Petah Tikva in the north and Beersheba in the south was filled with settlements.

The expansion of the population involved major water projects, including the National Water Carrier, as well as impressive achievements in Israeli agriculture. At the same time industry developed, a wide-ranging network of cultural and scientific institutions was established and the foundations were laid for a democratic regime – the only one in the entire Middle East thus far.

Among the uniquely difficult problems facing Israel was that of its identity – and its ties with the Jewish people throughout the world. This problem was expressed in many ways: the state is called Israel, the people are Jewish, the national movement is defined as Zionist, and the historical language – the Holy Tongue, made into a living language again, is Hebrew. How do these links fit together? How to preserve the delicate fabric – which was created over such long periods of oppression in which only religious tradition bound all together – in the new reality, and most especially in the world of the end of the 20th century, in which so much is in flux?

The answers are not easy. In any event, experience teaches us that the very existence of the State of Israel straightened the back of each Jew in every place in the world. Furthermore, any concern for Israel's continued existence aroused fear among Jews throughout the world.

Nor are the anxieties insignificant. Even after the War of Independence, the sword could not be returned to its scabbard; cease-fires did not turn into peace treaties; the threats by Israel's neighbors and the Arab boycott and siege became an inseparable part of Israel's life, and from time to time the fire burst forth.

In 1967, on Israel's 19th Independence Day, the Arab armies began to take various threatening steps which eventually resulted in the Six Day War. By its end, on June 11, 1967, Israel held all of western Eretz Israel. The noose which had

The Israel Defense Forces mobilized to play a significant role in the absorption of the mass immigration – familiarizing young immigrants with Israel's way of life among other things, by providing Hebrew classes such as the one advertised above.

been pulled so tight around its neck was slashed to ribbons in a victory unparalleled in history. But six years later the Yom Kippur War had to be fought, a war paid for in many lives, though it demonstrated Israel's strength and the inability of the Arab states to win on the battlefield. Only after it, did one begin to hear in the region sounds of coming to terms with the existence of Israel. Only afterwards did the chances for peace increase.

That, of course, is not the end. Let us return to what Herzl wrote at the beginning of the century: "Dreaming is a pleasant way for us to spend our time on earth. Dreams and reality are not as different as people tend to believe, for all man's deeds are based on dreams and will return to dreams."

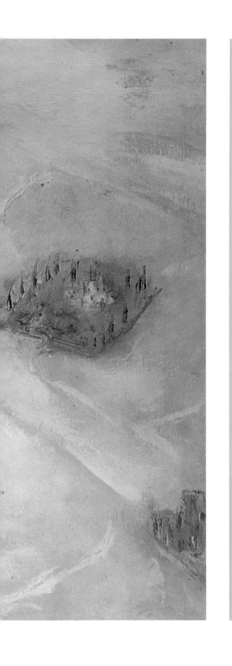

Jerusalem
City
of Faith

"Eretz Israel," we read in the **Talmud**, "is the hub of the world and its center. And Jerusalem is in the center of Eretz Israel, and the Temple is in the middle of Jerusalem, and the Holy of Holies is in the middle of the Temple, and the Ark is in the middle of the Holy of Holies, and the Foundation Stone – from which the world was made – in front of the Holy of Holies."

And the **Zohar** states:

"When the Holy One, blessed be He, created the world, He took a rock from underneath His throne of glory and threw it into the abyss. One side of that rock He planted in the abyss and the other side above. And that is at the middle of the world. From it the world expanded to the right and to the left and to all sides. That rock was created from fire and air and water, and all these froze and became a single rock which stands in the abyss. That stone is called the Foundation Stone, for from it the earth was founded. From that rock, the earth expanded in three stages: in the first, everything which was pure and delicate was placed on the earth; in the second, things were not as pure and delicate as in the first, but they were still pure and the dust was finer than the other dust in the world; in the third, the dust was dark and coarser than all the others, and around it lie the waters of the ocean which surround the entire world. Thus that point is at the very center, and everything which expanded in the world is around it."

While these quotations do not contain exact scientific or geographical truth, they have considerable spiritual, religious

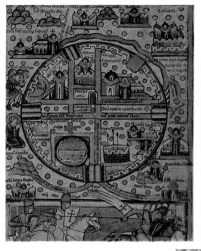

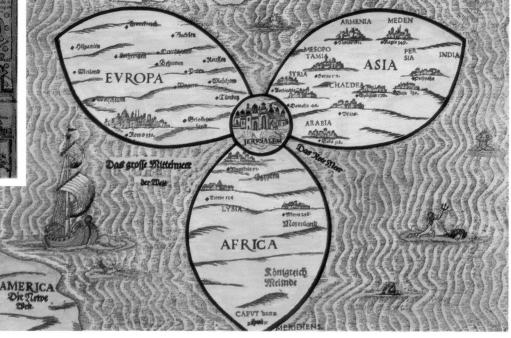

and cultural validity. The eternal capital of the Jewish people wherever they may live, the capital of Eretz Israel and of the State of Israel, is indeed, in many ways the hub of the universe. In the End of Days, Judgment Day, the prophet Isaiah promised, all nations will stream to it, and from it, the word of God will emanate to the entire world. But both in the past and in the present it has been and is in the minds of people everywhere. In the far north, in the distant west, in the thick of the African jungle, across the ocean, in the largest cities and the smallest villages, Jerusalem's name echoes, evoking emotion, some conscious and some not. There are those who only know it as "the Jerusalem that is Above": an entity which relates to God's kingdom in Heaven and bears no relation with the trials of everyday. Others, seeing it as "the Jerusalem that is below," pay anxious attention to its welfare, and are familiar with its geography and its holy places, the streets and alleys once walked upon by prophets and kings, conquerors and dreamers, philosophers and visionaries.

Even though thousands of years have passed since the days of King David and countless words have been written about the Jerusalem which he placed on the map of history, there can be no better summary of all that this city represents than the Psalm which reads: "A song of ascents/ of David./ I rejoiced when they told me/ Let us go to the House of the Lord./ Our feet stood/ In your gates, O Jerusalem./ Jerusalem is built as a city compacted together./ Where the tribes go up/ the tribes of the Lord, to the

"... David took the stronghold of Zion: the same is the city of David." That stronghold was probably next to the southern wall of the Temple Mount, but somehow belief persisted that it was actually located in the north-west corner of the Old City, where in the first century B.C.E. Herod had built a palace. The turret (above) became known as David's Tower.

Testimony of Israel/ to give thanks to the name of the Lord./ For there are set thrones of judgment,/ the thrones of the house of David./ Pray for the peace of Jerusalem/ They shall prosper that love you./ Peace be within your walls, and prosperity within your palaces./ For my brethrens' and companions' sakes/ I will now say, Peace be within you./ Because of the House of the Lord our God/ I will seek your good."

The City of David

Jerusalem has remained in that place – sometimes in glorious splendor, at other times crushed and in ruins – for five thousand years without interruption, and in this, too, it claims uniqueness. Mentioned for the first time – at least insofar as we know – in documents discovered at Ebla, southern Syria, that date back to the 3rd millennium B.C.E., it is called "Shalem," which is also one of the ways it is referred to in the Bible. And mentioned again in the Egyptian Execration Texts (of the beginning of the 2nd millenium B.C.E.), and in the Tel El-Amarna Letters (of the 14th century B.C.E.). as Urusalim. About a hundred years later, when Joshua bin Nun led the Israelite entry into Eretz Israel, he was confronted, among others, by Adonizedek, king of Jerusalem.

Looking back, it is easy to understand why the city arose where it did. First, all four elements needed for an ancient city were present: natural fields in open valleys (where wheat could be grown to produce bread); the Gihon spring (which

111

supplied in excess of 1,000 cubic meters of water each day, and which was enough for all the people and animals in the city); an important crossroads along major highways (on the mountain crest which stretches along the north-south axis and on the east-west axis from the coastal plain to the Jordan valley); and security (i.e., the possibility of locating a settlement near a water source and on a defensible route, given the weapons of those days). All of these contributed to Jerusalem being built on a small mountain, between the valley on one side and the Kidron river on the other.

It was here that King David arrived in 999 B.C.E., after having had his throne in Hebron for the first six years of his reign. He besieged and captured the city, as we are told: "David dwelled in the fort, and called it the city of David. And David built from Millo and inward. And David went on and grew great, and the Lord God of hosts was with him." Immediately afterwards he moved the capital to Jerusalem, first because of all the advantages mentioned above, and second, because it bordered on the mighty tribe of Judah while itself being in the territory of the small tribe of Benjamin – in other words, a place upon which all the other tribes could also agree. David's conquest was the sign for a dramatic change in Jerusalem's status, and within two years the change was cemented by the bringing of the Ark of the Covenant to Jerusalem. Now the capital became the spiritual and religious center of the Jewish people.

Twenty-four years after this, David paid fifty silver shekels for the threshing floor of Araunah the Jebusite on a mountain to

Solomon's Pools (right). This reservoir near Bethlehem was for hundreds of years an important component of the water conduit system extending from Mount Hebron to Jerusalem. (left) The hill separating David's City from the Temple Mount and called Ophel (or Millo), where Solomon built an entire complex of state offices and halls.

the north of the city, "and David built an altar there." Later, Solomon, David's son, would build the Temple in that place. The threshing floor of Araunah would become the Temple Mount, this, according to the Bible, being the mountain "in the land of Moriah" where the sacrifice of Isaac took place. Between this mountain and David's city there would be the Ophel, an elevated part of the city. To the west, the upper city would be constructed, and it would contain the royal palace, the women's quarters, the royal armory and other such buildings.

Over the years the city would expand; an excellent system would be built to supply water (as the original Shiloah tunnel and thereafter Hezekiah's tunnel show); it would see the towers built by Uzziahu and the reforms introduced by Jehoshaphat and Josiah; would overcome invaders such as Shishak, king of Egypt, and Sennacherib, king of Assyria; and would be the place where the great prophets would preach. In its courtyards, Isaiah ben Amotz would cry out: "How has the faithful city become a harlot! It was full of judgment; righteousness lodged in it; but now murderers." Jeremiah would call to it: "Wash your heart from wickedness, that you may be saved." And Joel would link his prophecy about the return from exile to Jerusalem: "I will also gather all nations, and will bring them down into the valley of Jehoshaphat, and will plead with them there for My people and for My heritage Israel, whom they have scattered among the nations, and they divided My land."

In 586 B.C.E., Jerusalem was destroyed by

Zachariah's grave, one of the ornate tombs quarried at Nahal Kidron for Jerusalem's upper classes in Second Temple times, was attributed by Jewish tradition to the Prophet Zechariah.

Nebuchadnezzar, the king of Babylon, and his captain of the guards, Nebuzaradan. The Temple, the royal palace and all the houses of Jerusalem were burned to the ground. The nation went into exile, but took an oath; "If I forget you, O Jerusalem, let my right hand forget its cunning, let my tongue cleave to my palate if I do not remember you, if I do not mention Jerusalem at the height of my joy."

Fifty years passed, and the prophet called out: "'Comfort you, comfort you, my people,' says the Lord. Speak to Jerusalem's heart and cry unto her, that her warfare is over, that her iniquity is pardoned, for she has received of the Lord's hand double for all her sins." The proclamation by Cyrus, king of Persia, permitting the Jews to return to Eretz Israel and to re-establish the Temple in Jerusalem was met with joy, and 42,000 people made the arduous trip back, where they began rebuilding the city and the Temple.

The Second Temple was completed in the year 516 B.C.E., but it did not have the grandeur of the First, possibly because of the troubled times. Thus the prophet Haggai had to turn to "Zerubabel ben Shealtiel the governor of Judea and to Joshua ben Jehozadak the high priest and to the remnants of the nation" and say to them: "Who is left among you that saw this house in its first glory? And how do you see it now? Is it not in your eyes in comparison of it as nothing? 'Yet now be strong, O Zerubbabel,' says the Lord; 'and be strong, O Joshua, son of Jehozadak, the high priest; and be strong, all you people of the land' ... For thus says the Lord of hosts ... 'The glory of this latter house shall be greater than of the former ... and in this place will I give peace.' "

And indeed, the Second Temple lasted longer than had the First, and for most of the time served as the center for the entire nation.

The City of the Sages

Jerusalem of the Second Temple is the Jerusalem of Ezra, who assumed the burdens of education and of building a renewed Jewish society. It is also the Jerusalem of Nechemiah, who expanded its territory, built its walls, placed six gates in them, and made a fortress to protect the city from attacks from the north.

Jerusalem of the Second Temple era is the Jerusalem of the Hellenizers, who tried to make the people accept the Hellenist culture in full and who established the "Antiochia of

"If I forget you, O Jerusalem: let my right hand forget its cunning." The vow made by the Babylonian Exiles, and which comes from the Book of Psalms, could be found in many Jewish homes.

Robinson's Arch, named for Edward Robinson, the distinguished 19th century American archeologist who discovered its remains, was the world's first interchange – built by Herod's engineers to give thousands of pilgrims access to prayer on the Temple Mount.

צורת   הבית

Jerusalem" in the shadow of the Hakra fortress.

Jerusalem of the Second Temple era is the Jerusalem of the Hasmoneans, a priestly family from the small village of Modi'in in the Lydda plain, which raised up the banner of revolt against the Seleucid king and against the attempt to obliterate the uniqueness of Judaism. Their daring, their skill and their zeal conquered Jerusalem and purified the Temple (in 164 B.C.E.), reconquering it (in 152), and re-establishing Jewish sovereignty (in 142) – at first under an ethnarch and then under a king.

Jerusalem of the Second Temple era is the Jerusalem of the Torah scholars known as **Chazal** (the acronym for the Hebrew expression, "our sages, of blessed memory"), of the Great Assembly and the Sanhedrin. This was the Jerusalem of the intellect, of thinkers, of the formulation of laws to ensure justice and enforce it, of profound concern for education. It was within this framework that Simeon the Just

formulated his statement that "the world survives on three things: Torah study, service (i.e., prayer), and helping others." It was also within this framework that Simeon ben Shetah instituted a compulsory education law – the first in history.

And Jerusalem of the Second Temple era is also the Jerusalem of Herod (37-4 B.C.E.), the city of which it was said: "He who did not see Jerusalem in its glory never in all his days saw a beautiful city." These were times of the spiritual flowering of great teachers and thinkers like Hillel and Shammai, whose repute was such that they needed no titles; of Rabbi Johanan and his disciples; and, too, times of economic growth that brought about unprecedented construction.

The glory of Jerusalem was the Temple, which Herod had renovated and much expanded. "It is said," the Talmud states, "that one who had never seen Herod's building had never seen a beautiful building in all his days. Of what did he build it? Rava said: 'Of yellow and white marble,' while others said, 'Of blue, yellow and white marble,' with alternate rows of stones projected, so as to leave a place for cement. He wished to plate them with gold, but the sages told him: 'Leave it, for this is more beautiful, like waves in the sea.'"

We know from archaeological and historical studies that Jerusalem numbered 150,000 people then, and that the gates of the Temple were opened on festive occasions to 100,000 pilgrims. Orchestrated by Herod, the Temple Mount area became the largest open square of antiquity, its size involving complex engineering and architectural innovations, with overpasses to relieve the pressure of traffic (relics of this still remain, as, for example, in Robinson's Arch), underground entrance tunnels, and gigantic gates.

The immense courtyard of the Temple Mount was supported on all four sides by retaining walls. As long as the Temple remained intact, they were not considered to possess special sanctity, but after the destruction of the Temple these walls still stood, and the western wall became sanctified by the Jewish people as the last vestige of the Temple – both for its grandeur and because the Talmud states that "the Western Wall of the Temple will never be destroyed – for the divine presence is in the west."

The City of three Religions

Before the destruction of the Temple, Jerusalem served as the birthplace of Christianity. In the third decade of the Common Era, Jesus ben Joseph, of the Jewish city of Nazareth in Galilee, arrived in Jerusalem to protest against the injustice and corruption that had spread both among the people and among those in the Temple itself. In his anger, he foretold the destruction of the city and the Temple, and was warmly acclaimed by the downtrodden and those seeking the way. Many of them became his disciples, regarding him as the Messiah. At the same time, he increasingly disturbed the conservative Jewish leadership, with his call for changes in the Jewish religion which Jewish tradition was unable to accept. At first, the High Priest and the heads of the Sanhedrin tried to persuade him to retract; failing, they demanded that the Roman governor, Pontius Pilate, try Jesus for subversion. In the end, the governor sentenced him to death, and he was crucified, as was the

The Cathedral of St James in Jerusalem's Armenian Quarter (opposite), built in the eleventh century on the ruins of a sixth century Byzantine church, is considered one of the country's lovliest churches. (below) The Via Dolorosa, as Ephraim Lilien drew it in 1912 as a New Testament illustration.

118

The Armenian
Quarter is in the
south-west of
Jerusalem's Old City.
The monastery at its
center (above right)
became Armenian in
the 13th century.
Residents of the
Quarter are known
for their traditional
pottery.

custom in those days – evidently during Passover in 30 C.E.
From that time on a new religion, Christianity, developed,
one which drew masses of people to it and was to
completely change the west and its culture. Thus Jerusalem,
the city in which Jesus had preached, in which, according to
Christian belief, he performed miracles, in which he was
crucified and where he was buried, contains sites holy to this
faith: Bethany to the east of the city, where Jesus revived
Eleazar; the cave on the Mount of Olives where he foresaw
the destruction of the city; the place of the Last Supper on
Mount Zion; Gethsemane, where he was seized by the
Roman soldiers; the Via Dolorosa, along whose entire length
he carried the cross; Golgotha, where he was crucified and
buried, and where Empress Helena erected the Church of
the Holy Sepulcher (there are those who think that this took
place at what is known as the Garden Tomb); and the place
where he ascended to heaven, on the Mount of Olives.

So the name of Jerusalem is an inseparable part of the vocabulary of believing Christians. Later, Christian pilgrims would come, following in the footsteps of Jesus; monks who wished to fulfill vows of abstinence; missionaries seeking to convert souls to Christianity; and the Crusaders – an army raised in Europe to redeem the tomb of Jesus from the hands of the heretics and set up the Kingdom of Jerusalem by means of blood and the sword.

In 638 C.E., more than 600 years after Jesus' crucifixion, Caliph Omar Ibn-Kattab conquered Jerusalem under the green flag of Islam, which had just been founded, a conquest that ushered in the Muslim era (which would continue until 1099) of the city and the country, and Jerusalem received a new name, "Madinat Al Makdas" (City of the Temple – meaning the Jewish Temple, of course), which would, in the course of time, be transformed into Al Kuds – the Holy. Soon the city would be linked to Muslim tradition, based on one short and cryptic reference in the Koran. There, we are told that the prophet Mohammed had to go to the "outer mosque" (Al-Aksa), which is not mentioned specifically as such, and then galloped into the heavens on a winged animal named Al-Buraq, with the body of a horse, the face of a woman, and the tail of a peacock.

"And his feet will stand in that day upon the Mount of Olives which is before Jerusalem on the East." A view of Jerusalem from the East by the British 19th century artist David Turner.

When he arrived at the mosque, he tethered his animal and was called on high, in the company of Abraham, Moses, and Jesus, to discuss matters regarding the law and prayer, and to prove that Islam, of all the monotheistic religions, was the true religion.

The Temple Mount was chosen as the site for these events. A site near the Golden Gate (and since the previous century, next to the Western Wall) is considered by Muslims to be the place where Al-Buraq was tethered. In the southern part of the courtyard, the Al-Aksa mosque was built, and the entire area near it declared holy ground. To emphasize the claim, in 691 Caliph Abd Al Malik built the magnificent Dome of the Rock. From then on, Jerusalem was a holy city for the three monotheistic religions of the west – Judaism, Christianity and Islam.

But for the Jews it was and is the only holy city. Only they face it in their prayers three times a day; only they, in all their diasporas, mourn its destruction, and conclude the prayers on the holiest day of their year, **Yom Kippur**, with the words, "I remember, O Lord, and I am amazed, as I see each city standing on its foundations, while the city of God is humiliated and brought to the lowest grave," and conclude the Passover **seder** meal with "Soon, with rejoicing, lead the offshoots of the stock You have planted, redeemed, to

The Dome of the Rock built by Caliph Abd el-Malik in the middle of the Temple Mount – as the British artist David Roberts (above) saw it in the 19th century. Erected around 690 C.E, the mosque is generally regarded as one of the world's architectural wonders.

Zion." And they continue to make pilgrimages to Jerusalem and to settle in it, and again to settle in it after having been uprooted, and in spite of all the difficulties involved. They returned to it after the Temple was destroyed and after Hadrian had turned it into Aelia Capitolina. In 362 C.E. they laid plans to revitalize it, after Emperor Julian the Apostate had ruled in Rome for three years and had attempted to halt Christianity. They helped the Persians conquer it from the Byzantines in 614. They blossomed there during the Fatimid dynasty, even establishing a major yeshivah, which served as a focus of their prestige and pride and as a source for rulings on Jewish law. They helped to defend Jerusalem from the Crusaders, and after Saladin occupied it in 1187 they were back. In 1267, under Nahmanides, they revived the community, and ever since there has been no break in the chronicle of Jewish life in Jerusalem.

In 1517, the Ottoman Sultan Selim conquered the city. Twenty-one years later his son, Suleiman the Magnificent, built – among other things – the wall around Jerusalem, the most exquisite of all city walls built in the 16th century. Suleiman's grandfather, Sultan Bayazid, had opened the gates of the Ottoman Empire to the Jews expelled from Spain. His grandson followed in his footsteps, encouraging Jews to settle in Jerusalem, and had the Western Wall area refurbished so that it could serve as a site for prayers.

"The Ruin ("Hurva") of Rabbi Yehuda He-Hassid" (above), the synagogue built in Jerusalem's Jewish Quarter between 1856 and 1864 with donations from Jews all over the world, on the ruins of an earlier synagogue built in 1705 and destroyed 16 years later. For a long time it served as a center for Jews throughout Eretz Israel, until it too was destroyed in the War of Independence.

It was then that the Jewish Quarter was established in Jerusalem. It numbered thousands of people, although the number varied at different times, depending on the circumstances. The Jews there built synagogues and study halls and absorbed the respective waves of immigration, surviving primarily on donations from abroad.

The New City

At the beginning of the 19th century, Jerusalem was the capital of a small district of the Damascus province of the Ottoman Empire. Insignificant, its economic activity was limited, its physical state deplorable, the Jews within it numbering some 2,000 out of a total population of about 9,000. But by the end of the first third of that century, a change was noticeable in the city's status. After Mohammed Ali conquered it in 1831, its gates were opened to the world at large, much construction got underway, and the situation of the Jews improved. Groups of immigrants from Europe

Nahlat Shivah (above, right and left), the third settled Jewish Quarter to be built outside Jerusalem's walls. Its name commorates the seven Jews from the Old City who bought the land in 1869. (below) The emblem of the Bezalel Art Academy, founded in 1906 by the Jewish artist Boris Schatz.

swelled the Jewish population, as did refugees from Safed fleeing that city after a major earthquake there. In 1836 the Jewish population already numbered 3,250, and within four years it had reached about 5,000, so that Jews represented the largest single group in Jerusalem.

At the same time, European involvement in Jerusalem increased; the consulates established in it offered protection and support for the Jews. As a result, Jewish capital flowed into the city, many houses were built in the Jewish Quarter, synagogues were completed, and public institutions founded. By 1870 there were 11,000 Jews in the city, a minority of these living in the neighborhoods which had begun to sprout outside the walls of the Old City. These included **Mishkenot Sha'ananim** (founded in 1860), **Mahaneh Yisrael** (1868), and **Nahalat Shivah** (1868). A short time later, **Me'ah She'arim** would be built, to be followed by **Yemin Mosheh, Sha'arei Hessed** and **Mahaneh Yehudah**. It was now that Jewish Jerusalem saw the founding of important educational institutions, including new schools. Printing presses were imported, newspapers began appearing. A new element came into existence: moderate **Maskilim** ("men of enlightenment"), who sought to produce social and cultural changes, including Abraham Moses Lunz, a pioneer in the study of Eretz Israel in the modern era; Eliezer Ben-Yehudah, who revived the Hebrew language; and community leaders such as Yehiel Michel Pines and David Yellin.

The Jewish national movement which arose at the end of the 19th century was first known as **"Hibbat Zion"** and afterwards as Zionism – Zion being one of the names of Jerusalem. Some of the immigrants who arrived were members of these movements who settled in Jerusalem and made a marked impact on it. By the beginning of World War I, in 1914, 45,000 Jews lived in Jerusalem, half of all the Jews in the country.

On December 11, 1917, a major historical change took place. As World War I neared its close, 401 years of Ottoman occupancy also came to an end. The British General Allenby entered Jaffa Gate on foot. "The large bell in Westminster Abbey tolled for the first time in three years. All the bells of the churches in Rome tolled for a full hour," wrote Allenby's biographer, recalling the emotion this step had aroused all over the world.

A few months later, Allenby took part in the laying of the cornerstone for the Hebrew University in Jerusalem, on Mount Scopus. Another seven years would pass until the university finally opened its doors, but it was quite clear that the Zionist movement saw Jerusalem as the capital of the Jewish national home and the modern spiritual center of the Jewish people. To emphasize this, Jerusalem was made the seat of the Zionist Executive, which led to "the state in the making."

Incidentally, Herzl, in his utopian novel, **Altneuland**, had written about rebuilding the Temple. Jewish tradition and Jewish law have left this task to be accomplished come the messianic era, while in the meantime the Jews struggled against both the British administration and the Muslim leadership for the right to pray next to the Western Wall, a struggle that also formed an element in the bloody events of 1929.

The Jewish community in Jerusalem grew and took firmer root, primarily in the new city. Even though there was a clear

The Hebrew University in Jerusalem, inaugurated on Mount Scopus in 1925, had to go into "exile" elswhere in the city during the War of Independence, only being able to return to Scopus after the Six Day War (above).

"The Ethiopians' Gate," Jerusalem – water-color by the Israeli painter Yossef Zaritsky.

Jewish majority, every attempt to find a political solution in Eretz Israel threatened to blow up over the problem of Jerusalem. The various plans for partition of the country left it outside the borders of the proposed Jewish state, as did the partition plan adopted by the U.N. General Assembly on November 29, 1947. This left Jerusalem in the midst of the

Arab state, under international supervision. The Arabs, who did not accept this plan, immediately embarked on unceasing attacks on the roads leading to the city, in the hope of cutting it off from the rest of Israel and starving it into surrender. But the Jewish community of Eretz Israel acted in the spirit of the words of David Ben-Gurion: "The value of Jerusalem cannot be measured or weighed or counted, because if a country has a soul, Jerusalem is the soul of Eretz Israel. The struggle for Jerusalem is decisive, and not only militarily .. Jerusalem demands and is entitled to have us stand by it ... Our enemies know that the fall of Jerusalem would be a mortal blow to the Jewish people. We have to enable Jerusalem to hold out for a lengthy period of time, even if it is under siege."

Indeed, the battles for Jerusalem and the territory around it represented a sizable part of the total Jewish effort in the War of Independence, cost many lives and brought great suffering to the city's residents. During this time, the Jewish Quarter of the Old City fell to the Tranjordanian Arab Legion and its residents were taken prisoner. Another aspect of the war was the cutting of the road leading from the coastal plain to Jerusalem and the forging of new roads to replace the original one.

On April 3, 1949, a cease-fire was signed between Israel and Transjordan, under the terms of which Jerusalem was divided, with barbed wire, concrete walls and land mines separating the two parts of the city. The entire Old City and the Mount of Olives remained outside Israel; Mount Scopus stayed a Jewish enclave. The agreement provided for a change of guard every two weeks for those stationed on Mount Scopus and for free access to the Western Wall, but the latter condition was never honored.

For nineteen years the city remained divided. At the beginning there was still the threat of internationalization. To prevent this, Jerusalem was proclaimed the capital of Israel and the major governmental functions were transferred to it. The President's Residence and the Knesset were both located there, as were most government ministries and the Supreme Court, the Israel Museum, Mount Herzl (where Herzl's bones had been reburied), the Yad Va-Shem national memorial to the victims of the Holocaust, and the Israel Academy of Sciences.

The city kept growing along the border, but was not recognized as Israel's capital by many nations of the world.

The forcing open of the road to Jerusalem and the raising of the Arab seige choking that city form a chapter of their own in the annals of the War of Independence – in which a dramatic role was played by the finding and clearing of the secret "Burma Road" (above) as an alternative route from the coastal plain.

Opposite: Jerusalem, a vivid, modern city, not only a holy one.

The Knesset, in the heart of the Ben-Gurion complex in Jerusalem (above), living symbol of Jerusalem as the capital city of the State of Israel.

Major reconstruction of the Jewish Quarter in the Old City (opposite), destroyed in 1948, was launched with the war's end in 1967. From then on, total freedom of worship has reigned in Jerusalem, as depicted (insert) in the picture from a recent "Children Draw Jerusalem" exhibition.

In May 1967, the deteriorating situation in the Middle East led to the Six Day War. When the war broke out on June 5, the Israeli government warned the king of Jordan not to intervene, but his troops began to bombard Israeli Jerusalem. There was no choice but to react; within two to three days Israeli forces occupied the entire territory which had been held by the Jordanians west of the Jordan, including the eastern part of Jerusalem. On June 7, 1967, the army command heard over its communication system, "The Temple Mount is in our hands"; Israeli paratroopers stormed to the Western Wall, and at last it was open to Jews. Jerusalem was again joined together. The different obstacles were removed. Mount Scopus was no longer an enclave. The Jewish Quarter in the Old City was again populated by Jews. Freedom of worship was ensured for all. For the past twenty-five years Jerusalem has been the focus of development and construction, of widespread archeological studies into its glorious and exciting past – and of human

and political confrontations. The Arab population has not yet accepted the city's unification, and in the world at large there are still many who question it. But it is hard to imagine that the city will again be divided, that a border will once more cut the city in two.

For those who seek its welfare and love it, for the Jewish people who have yearned for it and carried it in their hearts for so long, one can only hope and pray: "May there be peace in your fort, tranquility in your palaces."

The Israel Experience

Israel is a multi-faceted country – historically (as already mentioned in earlier chapters), geographically and in terms of the way people live. It has mountains which are more than a thousand meters high, and an enclosed lake – the Dead Sea – which is four hundred meters below sea level. It has a wide spectrum of flora, with more than 2,600 species growing in forests, groves, semi-arid land and desert. It has sand and basalt, a fascinating geology and extraordinary archaeology.

And it has renowned scientific institutions and places which are holy to three religions (and to small splinter groups), nuclear reactors and flocks of sheep, modern farming methods along with knowledge-intensive industries and a highly developed bureaucracy, colorful fruit and vegetable markets and stimulating book fairs, crowded highways and nature preserves, a garbled mixture of planning and improvisation, with reliance on miracles and luck.

A quick look reveals the most modern western technology along with clearly Middle Eastern sights, religious and non-religious, soldiers and civilians, skin and eye colors ranging the full gamut of mankind, tailored suits and open-necked shirts, a thousand and one kinds of music, culinary dishes of all types. A more serious look will show that Israel is indeed part of the "global village" of the communications era, along with numerous examples of provincialism, serious differences of opinion along with national pride, and an unending discussion about questions of identity.

Either way, between all the extremes mentioned above, there are many intermediate stages, and among these there are certain basic characteristics which are worth commenting on individually.

The Ingathering of the Exiles

Israel is a country of immigrants. Most Israeli Jews were born in Israel, and within the country a culture and way of life have developed and are developing which are intimately linked to its landscape and to local conditions. And yet, wherever one turns, there are the vivid signs of the immigration which has come from the four corners of the earth, representing seventy countries and tongues. True, there has been a continuous Jewish presence in Eretz Israel ever since the Twelve Tribes conquered the land in the second half of the thirteenth century B.C.E., and that there has been a steady immigration of Jews to it ever since the destruction of the Second Temple (in 70 C.E.). But mass immigration only began at the end of the last century, with the First Aliyah (Hebrew for "ascent") a wave which began in 1882. It follows then that only a very small percentage of those living in contemporary Israel boast ancestors tracing back in Eretz Israel for five or more generations. All others, even if they themselves did not immigrate to the country, are the children, grandchildren, or great-grandchildren of immigrants.

Let us look, for example, at the origins of high-ranking government officials in 1986-1987. Israel's president was an immigrant from Ireland; the Knesset Speaker – an immigrant from Iraq; the Prime Minister and the alternate Prime Minister – both immigrants from Poland; one of the Deputy Prime Ministers – a descendant, on his father's side, of a family which has lived in Jerusalem for many generations; the other – an immigrant from Morocco. Fourteen Ministers born in Israel were the children of immigrants; another six Ministers were immigrants from Yugoslavia, Iran, the United States, Morocco and Germany; the Chief Justice of the Supreme Court was an immigrant from Danzig; the IDF Chief of Staff – an immigrant from Iraq; and the Chief of Police – an immigrant from Hungary.

It is important to stress that in Jewish tradition immigrating to Eretz Israel is more than merely moving there; it is also, for the most part, an act of religious and spiritual significance, the expression of the longing for redemption,

"And he...shall assemble the outcasts of Israel and gather together the dispersed from the four corners of the earth." (Opposite, above/left) Russian immigrants 1922; (Above right) Immigrants from Salonika at the end of the 19th century; (Below) A wedding dance of Libyan immigrants; (Center) Immigrants from Samarkand, seen by the lyric poet Else Lasker-Schueler.

an echo of the ancient prayer of "gathering the scattered from among the other nations," the realization of the national yearning to return to the historic homeland. But even those who did not move to the country for exclusively ideological reasons are still not like ordinary immigrants elsewhere (even if they have to contend with the problems which they would face in any other country).

The difference lies in the place of Aliyah in the national roster of priorities – both before the establishment of the State and during all the years of the State's existence thus far. Jews living in Eretz Israel have always called upon other Jews to join them there, have longed for them to come, and

mobilized themselves – whatever the difficulties or penalties – to bring them to the country and absorb them. Despite all the problems and obstacles, there has always been a passionate collective effort to share with new immigrants whatever resources were or are available, and to make them feel, literally, at home as soon as possible.

One memorable example of this was the behavior of the Jews in Eretz Israel in the years of the "illegal immigration," between 1934 and 1948. At the time, the British Mandatory government effectively closed the gates of the country to Jewish immigration, and the Yishuv reacted to this by bringing in Jews "illegally," by every possible means – in broken down ships, through the desert, and even in planes which evaded the authorities.

Another example is to be found in Israeli legislation. The very first law enacted by the State of Israel repealed all earlier laws restricting the right of Jews to immigrate to Israel, a reference to this having been made earlier in Israel's Declaration of Independence. A short while later, the Law of Return was passed. Every Jew, so states the law, has the inherent right, by virtue of being a Jew, to come to Israel as an *oleh* – a new immigrant – and to receive Israeli citizenship. There are those who are opposed to the law, who decry its automatic aspects, but the vast majority of the Israeli public perceives it as an integral part of the State's existence and as the most fitting national response to the history of the Jewish people: no more quotas and barred gates, and thus no more immigrants – only *olim*.

The saga of Aliyah is the story of the 122,000 "illegal" *olim* who came by sea, land (including those who literally walked through the desert, from Iraq to Eretz Israel), and air. It is the story of the 102,000 *olim* who arrived in Israel between the Declaration of Independence, on May 14, 1948, and the end of that year, at the height of the battles of the War of Independence. And of another 583,000 who arrived by the end of 1951. Or the story of "Operation Magic Carpet," that flew in to Israel almost all the rest of Yemenite Jewry, and of "Operation Ezra and Nehemiah," which brought in almost all the Jews of Iraq, or of the Aliyah of hundreds of thousands from Poland and Romania, Morocco and Iran.

No less is it the story of the austerity regime that marked the first years of the State, so that the limited resources could be evenly divided among a population that had grown so rapidly; of temporary housing thrown up to meet the

Anxious eyes watch them come across the seas and deserts. (Opposite, above) Immigrants from Yemen, here near Aden, making their way to the Land on foot; (Below) The "Jewish State," with its "illegal" immigrants arriving from Bulgaria, October 1947. (Above right) The Hand-embroidered headgear Yemenite women reserved for very special occasions.

critical housing needs, that, though it provided shelter, was inevitably to create social problems, bring about confrontations between different groups forced into such close proximity despite dissimilar traditions, and result in factional political activity and charges of discrimination by those reared in these impoverished areas.

And in recent years it has also been the story of two electrifying waves of Aliyah, that from Ethiopia and that from the Soviet Union and its successor states.

The Ethiopian Jews, who were known as Falashas, are members of an ancient tribe calling itself Beta Israel. Its origins are still shrouded in mystery. Until 1948, only a few Ethiopians were able to leave for Eretz Israel, and at no time was there much immigration, given the complex relations between Israel and Ethiopia. But with the change of regimes in the country, the condition of the Falashas deteriorated and concern for their fate intensified. Hundreds, then thousands, left their villages, made their way to southern Sudan, going on from there in circuitous ways to Israel. Some of them were even taken by boat to ships of the Israeli Navy awaiting them in the Red Sea. In the winter of 1984, 10,000 Falashas lived in camps in southern Sudan. The move from there to Israel was a long process, but finally, at the end of that year, Israel embarked on "Operation Moses," flying 7,000 people, within a period of two months, via Europe to Israel. All in all, about 16,000 Falashas arrived in Israel during the 1980's, with a similar number still remaining in Africa.

In 1991 these were brought out, almost to a man, in "Operation Solomon." When it became clear that a new revolution was about to take place in Ethiopia and that the lives of the Falashas were again in danger, the Israeli government undertook a remarkable series of steps, including political contacts at the highest international levels, various highly unconventional deals, and a sensational airlift orchestrated by the Israeli Air Force, which flew almost all the remaining Jews of Ethiopia to Israel within two to three days, bringing a very long historical era to an end.

At the same time, the massive operation of bringing Jews to Israel from the Soviet Union was in full swing. The gates of their country had been sealed for decades, even before the Iron Curtain descended on Europe after World War II. The authorities in the Soviet Union had consistently and relentlessly pursued all manifestations of Jewish nationalism, suppressing any attempt to create a link between Jews and Israel. Matters reached such a state that the millions of Jews in the Soviet Union became known to the world as "the Jews of Silence," their voices unheard, they themselves unable to hear any voices from the outside. Despite this, the embers still flickered in the depths of their hearts, and their longing to settle in Israel never abated.

Following the Six Day War, pressure on the Soviet government increased. Throughout the world demonstrations demanded that the USSR open its gates, to "let my people go." Afterwards, various "refuseniks" came to

HOMEWARD BOUND   ALIYAH 90

the fore within the Soviet Union itself; men and women who were willing to risk imprisonment, the loss of careers, wages and property, and to be permitted to live in Eretz Israel. One such was Nathan (Anatoli) Scharansky, convicted – solely due to his desire to reach Israel – of treason against his country, of spying for the United States and of subversion, and who was sentenced in 1978 to thirteen years imprisonment. In the courtroom, he declared, "This coming year in rebuilt Jerusalem," and he did not suspend his struggle until he was released and made Aliyah at the beginning of 1986.

Three years later, the trickle became a flood. The international situation, and the collapse of the Soviet Union which had begun by then, caused a huge exodus of Soviet Jews to Israel – 200,000 in 1990, 175,000 in 1991, with many still on their way. In December 1990, Israel could celebrate the arrival of its two-millionth immigrant.

To absorb this mass was not and is not simple. The proportion of those already living in the country and doing the absorbing has changed radically since the early 1950's, the standard of living has grown, and the investment needed for immigrant absorption has also grown tremendously. Add to this problems of housing and employment, of acquiring a new language and changing one's lifestyle, and the process of adjustment that has always been required of Israel's newcomers.

But what matters most is what Israel's noted author A.B. Yehoshua wrote at the end of 1990: "This great Aliyah streaming to Israel is wonderful. I walk in the streets, meet these *olim* and feel that after a prolonged national hunger and thirst I am being nourished with milk and honey. The State of Israel is being inundated by something whose immense dimensions, I believe, it cannot yet grasp. All of us, *olim* and old-timers, are as if in a dream."

Making the Wasteland Bloom

In 1867, the first group of tourists to the Holy Land, organized by Thomas Cook, arrived in Eretz Israel. It included the famous American author, Mark Twain, who travelled throughout the land, and wrote on his experiences in his *Innocents Abroad*. His description is one of a land lying completely waste.

Thirty-one years after Mark Twain's visit to Eretz Israel, it was visited by the founder of the Zionist movement,

The return to working the land was an inseparable part of the Zionist dream. Jewish farm laborers on their way to the fields of the Hefer Valley in the 1930s. (inset), a Jewish National FUnd calendar honoring the 1920s "conquest," i.e. cultivation of the Jezreel Valley.

Theodor Herzl, who would later write, in his utopian novel, *Altneuland*, about two tourists, one Jewish, the other Christian, who undertake a short tour of the country: "The next morning ... they travelled ... to the agricultural settlements. They saw the settlements of Rishon Le-Zion, Rehovot and others, which were like oases in the midst of a desolate land. Many diligent hands had labored here, until the clods of earth had been reawakened. They saw fields tended properly, lovely vineyards, and orange orchards bursting with fruit. All of these, the head of the Jewish settlement of Rehovot explained to them, had arisen in the last ten or fifteen years."

Indeed, even if the authors quoted above were not entirely accurate in their descriptions of the actual situation, the fact is that between 1867 and 1898 a Jewish settlement movement had begun which involved making the wasteland bloom – and not by chance. The Jewish national movement dreamed not only of the revival of Jewish national sovereignty in Eretz Israel, but also of a return to the land and agriculture. The efforts to realize this dream were faced with many obstacles – from major problems in purchasing land, through swamps which spread malaria and shortages of water. But these obstacles did not halt the movement.

Opposite: (Above), the plastic hot houses of the Jordan Valley represent high-tech Israeli agriculture. (Below) The settlement of Kinneret, as it looked in 1937.

The Lahav forest marks the limits of the wilderness of Mount Hebron's western slopes.

Within a hundred years Israeli agriculture had earned many records on an international scale, and was growing enough to export vast quantities of produce. Even if much of the southern part of Israel, the Negev, has remained uncultivated, the other parts are covered by a widespread network of settlements. The swamps have been drained. A waterworks network, including the National Water Carrier, has enabled the cultivation of marginal land almost throughout the country. Close cooperation between farmers and scientists has produced new types of crops and sophisticated work methods. Peppers and avocados, melons, artichokes and flowers – and of course the famous Jaffa oranges – are flown or shipped from Israel to almost everywhere in Europe. At any one time, Israeli instructors can be found at work in developing countries in Africa, Latin America and the Far East – and they often do so without waiting for diplomats to formalize the relations between Israel and these countries. In short, this is a major success story.

The Kibbutz and the Moshav

The "assault" of the Jewish community of Eretz Israel on the wilderness and the speedy development of Israeli agriculture took place at a time filled with exciting social experiments,

In the background, a camel; in the forefront, jugs and a a barrel. The celebration of water at Kibbutz Urim in the Western Negev, shortly after its establishment in 1947.

reflected in other areas of the Israel experience.

In the beginning, the Halutzim ("pioneers") of the Second Aliyah wave, the idealistic people who arrived in Eretz Israel from Eastern Europe from 1903 on and wanted so much to be engaged in agricultural work, faced great difficulties. As they were idealists who were not used to physical labor, each day meant a fierce struggle. In an attempt to overcome their economic misery, many of them joined communes – small groups which lived a communal life, to one extent or another, a life style in keeping with their socialist views and their dreams of bettering human society. But years had to pass before they could articulate all this in ideological terms.

Before this happened, in 1910, an intense debate broke out between the communes whose members worked in a Zionist farm in the Jordan Valley and the farm's manager. Dr. Arthur Ruppin, in charge of Zionist settlement activity in those days, proposed that the members of the communes should try to run half the farm, east of the Jordan, by themselves. A year later, the experiment having worked, those who had conducted it decided to continue it. Ten single men and two single women now agreed to work together and to share everything ("From each according to his ability, to each according to his need") and to stress in

A major social experiment that got underway almost by accident – the first Kibbutz, Deganiah, as it was in 1910.

149

all aspects the importance of mutual aid. At first they thought that they would also forgo family life and child-bearing, but soon afterward they arrived at different conclusions. By the time the first couples married and had children, the place they lived in was already a settlement named Deganya.

At first they called this way of life a "kvutza" (group), and made sure that the group would remain small, a sort of family. Afterwards they embarked on further experiments, establishing large "kvutzot" (plural of "kvutza"), called kibbutzim. At this stage, after World War I, they already spoke of more carefully planned initiatives, in terms of social and ideological reforms and in regard to their duty to the nation. One theorist envisioned "a society which will ... open its arms to all those who have been defeated, who have been ostracized, who suffer." He also preached unlimited growth and the group's involvement in all areas of production and creativity. Others spoke of a mass settlement movement to serve as the major, almost exclusive method for the transferring of pioneers to Eretz Israel.

Over the years it became clear that the original dream of total equality could not be realized. Meanwhile, kibbutzim arose all over the country. It may very well be that the very social structure itself enabled kibbutzim to be established and to take possession of land wherever this was called for in the creation of the Zionist map. Their sense of cooperation, their pioneering spirit and their continuing concern for innovation, helped the kibbutz members to withstand adversity, cope with hardships and face dangers that, as individuals, they might well not have been able to endure.

The kibbutzim also served as the base for the formation of the Haganah – the defense arm of the Yishuv before the establishment of the State – and especially its mobilized units, the Palmah. The kibbutzim hid "illegal" immigrants, absorbed youth groups which had fled the Holocaust or belonged to economically depressed strata, and fostered, trained and mobilized emissaries for special projects in the service of the nation.

The kibbutzim also provided especially favorable conditions for the development of agricultural innovations. From the beginning, they adopted the most up-to-date methods, showing great flexibility in developing the economy, which

Opposite: From plough (Hasidim, 1937) to tractor, Israeli agriculture has been a remarkable success.

enabled them, in time, to move from an almost total dependence on agriculture, to industrial enterprises and services, and to establish, among others, state-of-the-art factories. The statistics are impressive: for example, in the mid-1980's, when the kibbutz population (in 271 kibbutzim) was about 3.5% of the Jewish population of Israel, kibbutzim produced 40% of all agricultural products, 6.5% of all industrial products, and 7.5% of industrial exports. The kibbutz society has long devoted substantial resources to education. For years, all children were raised together in special quarters, paralleling the sharing of other family functions (as, for instance, the kibbutz communal dining room), but over the past two decades most kibbutzim have moved to having children sleep in their parents' quarters, and the communal dining room has also diminished in importance.

Not least, the kibbutzim have been greatly involved in fostering cultural creativity, producing authors and artists, establishing publishing companies, and finding original and attractive ways to commemorate traditional holidays and festivals, such as the reaping of the first barley crop (the *omer*) of the season and bringing in the first fruits (*bikkurim*) of the year.

More than eighty years after the kibbutz movement was

launched, its future as a social experiment is still not clear;
many Israelis spent their formative years in kibbutzim, only
to decide eventually that the way of life was not for them –
and this includes members of the second, third and fourth
generations of the kibbutzim. The great Jewish philosopher,
Martin Buber, defined the entire kibbutz venture as "an
incredible non-failure," and there are those who still see it as
"an incredible success."

Within the kibbutz movement, however, there arose yet
another form of communal settlement, in which the degree
of cooperation is more limited – the "moshav ovdim," based
on an idea born in the second decade of the century,
among members of the Deganya and Kinneret kvutzot who
wanted more economic independence while yet being able
to enjoy the other benefits of sharing. Various settlements
sprang up based on family land holdings, in which the
members accepted three basic principles: no employment
of outside help, mutual aid, and cooperation in marketing
and in the purchase of the means of production.

"Moshavim" spread throughout the country, but their very
nature defined where they could be deployed and where
not, and to what extent they could be coopted to help in
community-wide tasks. There were, for instance, areas for
settlement suitable only for units based on collective

production, not on smallholdings worked individually. Furthermore, the moshav's economic division weakened the social ties among the members. It became increasingly difficult for the moshavim to preserve the principle of working only by themselves, their communal marketing created problems, and the level of mutual aid decreased. Furthermore, due to their family structure, they were less flexible than the kibbutzim in adapting to economic changes, and found it difficult, for example, to develop industries.

However, the moshavim also chalked up a number of successes. First and foremost, many served as the base for successful agricultural initiatives. Second, after 1948 the moshav was seen as a good social framework for the absorption of many *olim*, useful in dispersing the population and in increasing agricultural production. In the first decade of the State's existence, tens of new moshavim sprang up, extending over entire areas of the Negev, Galilee and Israel's eastern border.

Israeli Democracy

"We are both presidents," said Chaim Weizmann, the first President of Israel, to Harry Truman, the 33rd President of the United States. "You are the president of almost 200,000,000 people, and I am president of less than a million. But my job is harder. I am the president of a country where all the citizens are presidents." In this pithy comment, Weizmann depicted a situation also expressed in the saying that "Whenever there are two Jews, there are three political parties." In short, Israeli society is vibrant, its citizens showing a high degree of public and political knowledge and an interest in influencing their destiny.

As such, it is, of course, a democratic society, to the extent that this appears self-evident to Israel's citizens. But the story is not simple. Three basic facts must be mentioned in this regard: Israel, having achieved independence in the midst of a war, has been forced ever since to battle for its survival, has invested tremendous resources and energy in security; also, many of its citizens came to it from non-democratic countries – be they European or Asian or African; and finally, the first years of Israel's existence were hardly a golden era for democracy anywhere in the world, least of all in the Middle East. We need but note that in the 1950's there were still many who pledged their allegiance to

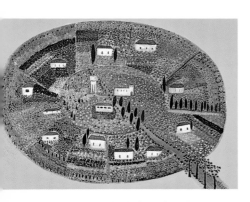

The "circle" of Nahalel (painted by Yehoshua Brandstatter) came to symbolize the moshav – an Israeli innovation that played an important part in the absorption of immigrants.

Opposite: Israeli democracy in action: The State's first President, Chaim Weizmann, casts his vote in the first Knesset elections. (Above, left); Notice boards buckle under the burden of campaign material. (Above, right); The Knesset in session. (Below).

An additional view of democracy – across-the-board public demonstrations by both right and left wing, Orthodox and secular groups, each attempting within legal limits to influence public opinion on major policy matters.

the gospel as preached by "the world of tomorrow" of totalitarian Moscow.

What mitigated much of the above was that Israel grew out of an organized community, established under the influence of a voluntary ideological movement, which, though it lacked all governmental powers to enforce "proper" conduct and unity, operated on the basis of widespread agreement – something unattainable without a democratic approach. This movement was also engaged in rebelling against the iron hand of the ruling (non-democratic) authorities of Eastern Europe, and was profoundly influenced by the national and liberal awakenings in the West. Added to this was the need to give expression to a nation whose very existence was in dispute.

And, in the background, stood the ancient Jewish tradition. This tradition had a central religious core, but it was imbued with democratic ideals. Judaism had neither pope nor caliph, but it gloried in the clear concepts of "give and take," "following the majority," and "the power of two witnesses to determine issues."

At the beginning of 1949, only seven months after the Declaration of Independence, the young State went to the polls – having already established an independent judiciary, including a Supreme Court which was authorized to act as

a High Court of Justice.

Since then, none have questioned the authority of the elected bodies of the State, and the importance of the rule of law has never been in doubt. Elections are run properly and at the correct times, governmental bodies abide by High Court of Justice injunctions, and decisions rendered by legally constituted commissions of enquiry are fully implemented, even when ministers or senior military officials must be removed from office.

Almost from its establishment, the Zionist movement, and in its wake Israeli society, was engaged in vehement arguments regarding the ideology and basic principles of Zionism. Time took care of some of these arguments, but others have cropped up to replace them. Today, the major internal disputes are related mostly to various ideas as to the future of the territories occupied by Israel in the Six Day War, to the social disparities, to the status of religion in the State, to the government's involvement in the economy, and to the structure of the government. Many of these often deep differences of opinion reflect divisions within the parties themselves, something that has in no small measure affected public discussion of the issues involved, often leading to extra-parliamentary activity which finds its expression in mass demonstrations and general ferment.

Looking back, it may perhaps be claimed that the partisan polarization has decreased. And yet, from time to time one hears talk of the Moment of Truth, of an explosive situation and of the need to decide once and for all. Every so often warnings are issued about danger to the future of democracy, and even of the possibility of a civil war. The past gives cause for hope that the doom-sayers are exaggerating greatly. Experience, though, shows that the immediate future will certainly not be boring. If we repeat Weizmann's words above, the number of "presidents" has just grown as the population has increased – and people's belief in their "presidency" has not waned.

The People's Army

There are those who say that the standing orders of the Israeli army include the following: "Privates will not offer advice to the Chief of Staff during times of war." If one wishes to relate to the question in a more serious manner, he can turn to the words of David Ben-Gurion, the first prime minister and defense minister of the State of Israel, in 1953, at a conference of senior army officers: "The army is not merely a military force in the narrow sense; it is also an educational tool of the nation during times of peace. It is not the only tool, but one of the major ones. The army must be a major factor, although not the only one, in shaping the profile of the nation, in merging those from different Diasporas, in educating the Jew who comes to us from the Diaspora, who does not know what the feeling of freedom is ... The army is the largest school we have in the country ... The first principle upon which the army is based is ties with the Jewish people throughout the world ... The second and most vital principle is that the nation and its decisions are supreme, that it is the nation's decision, and there must be acceptance by the army and by each individual within it of the nation's decision."

This has been true for the Israeli army ever since it was founded. When it was first established, it was named the Israel Defense Forces – stressing that its main goal is to defend the country – but its strategy has always been offensive, in order to drive the battle away from civilian population centers, which, in any event, are not far from the border. And yet, and maybe because of this, it is the people's army.

No logical individual can visualize a realistic scenario of a

David Ben-Gurion, the man who determined, when the State was established, that Israel's armed forces would be subject to the absolute control of a civilian government.

(Opposite) The comradeship of those who bear arms has typified the values of the Israel Defense Forces ever since their creation in 1948. (Inset) Soldiers of the Yiftah Brigade in Upper Galilee in the War of Independence, as depicted by Shmuel Katz.

June 7, 1967;
paratroopers at the
Western Wall, in
Jewish hands for the
first time since the
destruction of the
Second Temple

Opposite: Women
soldiers in the I.D.F.
serve in a wide range
of capacities,
including (Below) the
training of
youngsters.

military putsch in Israel. No Israeli general can lead his
soldiers into battle against the government, for the IDF is
not an independent entity. It is based on a long tradition of
volunteers who defended the Jewish population of Eretz
Israel before the establishment of the State, and even left it
to rescue threatened Jews outside the country.

The IDF is made up of two parts, both including the
population at large: the regular army which drafts all Israelis
who have reached the age of 18 – with young men serving
for three years, young women for two years; and the
reserve forces, which include all those who have completed
regular army service but stay in the reserves until they are
51. The latter have been defined as soldiers on leave for
eleven months of the year. Once a year, at least, all Israeli
men are called up for active service. It is they, therefore,
who form the bulk of the army in war. It is a fact, for
example, that the units which unified Jerusalem in the Six
Day War were all reserve units.

A debate has long raged within and around the IDF
regarding the appropriate degree of discipline and
ceremonial and the rigidity of the relationship between
officers and their troops. Many claim that the proper
formula has not yet been found, while others insist that it
was found and lost. Either way, experience teaches that

military service leaves its imprint on Israeli society as deeply as that society imprints the army. Without a doubt, the IDF, as a melting pot is unique; within its ranks, without any barriers of any kind, regardless of country of origin or class, the Israeli nation is forged and formed.

One can attribute this to the fact that the young generation spends an important segment of its formative years in army uniform. One can mention tension-filled days and nights of being on alert, in which the army staggers under the burden of cakes sent by the civilian population located close to army bases. One can single out the IDF educational system, which ensures, among others, that soldiers of lower socio-economic strata complete their elementary education, its operations when necessary encompassing growing vegetables, paving roads and the care of new *olim*. And one can also mention that the broadcast waves and the newspapers and the different public controversies do not stop at the fences of the different army bases.

This, then, is a people's army, but one which is also professional and trained. Many of its achievements and innovations are to be found in various battlefields and in books of military history. An example of this was Operation Yonatan. On June 27, 1976, Palestinian terrorists hijacked an Air France plane and flew it to Entebbe, Uganda, threatening to kill its more than 100 Israeli passengers. Instantly, the IDF prepared an audacious plan to free the hostages. Drilled down to the last detail, two hundred IDF soldiers boarded Air Force planes that flew them directly to Entebbe, some 2,500 miles from Israel's southern border. Landing safely without detection, the small force assaulted the airport, freed the Israelis, and flew them back to Israel, each flight taking about seven hours. Between the two flights, they were on the ground for ninety minutes, fifty of which went on fighting and freeing the hostages and forty on various preparations needed in order to take off. The world held its breath at the impeccable planning and implementation. Everyone also realized not only the length of the IDF's strong arm and its daring, but also its determination to protect Israeli citizens wherever they are.

The Minorities in Israel

About 18% of the 4.7 million citizens of Israel are non-Jews. Almost all of them are members of the Arab minority. Most of these are Sunni Muslims (including about 80,000 Druze), with a minority who are Christians of various groups (Greek Catholics, Greek Orthodox, Catholics, Maronites, Protestants and others). About a tenth (80,000) of the members of the minorities are Druze. One can also find among the minorities small groups of Circassians and Bahai.

Some of the members of these minorities were citizens of the State when it was declared. It was to them that a special call was directed in the Declaration of Independence: "to preserve peace and participate in the upbuilding of the State on the basis of full and equal citizenship and due representation in all the provisional and permanent institutions." This was a call which went on to "appeal – in the midst of the onslaught launched against us now for months," to indicate that the relations between Jews and Arabs in Eretz Israel and in the State of Israel are not divorced from the prolonged national struggle, one expressed in a number of wars, thousands of dead and an enormous amount of suffering and unpleasantness.

The preceding pages – a glimpse of Israel Defense Force training.

The Israel experience also involves far-reaching economic and social change for members of the State's non-Jewish minorities. (Opposite) (1) Nazareth dignitaries on the first Knesset election day. (2) The Beduin donkey must now give way to the car. (3,5) Representatives of some of the 35 different Christain sects. (4) Druze sheikhs in traditional headgear. (6) The Bahai Temple in Haifa.

1

2

5

3

4

6

"My State is in conflict with my people," said the late Al-Aziz al-Zuebi of Nazareth, a member of the Knesset for many years, describing the major strains in the life of the Arab citizens of Israel. Already in 1949 they had been given the right to vote for, and stand for election to, the Knesset, but until 1966 they were subject, to one extent or another, to the rule of a military government. Afterwards, though officially their status became the same as the State's other citizens, they were not fully absorbed in Israeli society, and indeed could hardly have been so, partly because the Arab-Israeli dispute has not yet ended, and partly because the Israeli Arabs themselves have shown no interest in giving up their own identity and assimilating among the Jews. Nevertheless, it is clear that they have been involved, over the past few years in a social and economic revolution; their patriarchal and tribal framework has been undermined, the Arab work force is employed increasingly in urban centers, Israeli social legislation has narrowed the gap between the different Arab classes; the young generation having become acquainted with new innovative life styles, has begun to shatter long-entrenched conventions. One of the clearest expressions of this upheaval is in the field of education: the Arab student population in the first forty years of Israel's existence has grown twenty-fold or more, while the Arab population as a whole has only grown five-fold in the same period.

We should also note that Arabic is an official language in Israel, and that there are numerous places holy to members of the minorities throughout the country – most in Jerusalem and some in the north. The latter include the Basilica of the Annunciation in Nazareth; the grave of Nebi Shu'eib, near the Horns of Hittin, sacred to the Druze; and the Bahai Temple in Haifa.

The Hebrew Revolution

The author Ephraim Kishon once stated that Israel is the only country where parents learn their mother tongue from their children. Beneath this exaggeration lies one of the remarkable achievements of the Jewish people in the last century: the revival of Hebrew from a tongue used only in the study of holy works to one used commonly in the market and the university, on the stage and on the football field.

The status of Hebrew as a spoken language was evidently

Opposite:
"Be-Teavón" means "Good Appetite!" in Hebrew. Watermelon (Above) and felafel (Below) rank high on the Israeli menu.

challenged close to the destruction of the Second Temple –
in the first century C.E. Ever since that time, it was used
almost exclusively in the study of the holy books and in
written communications. Jews, wherever they were, prayed
in Hebrew, even debated in it, but did not use it on a
day-to-day basis. They traded, calculated, loved and
dreamed in the languages of the countries in which they
lived or in mixed languages such as Yiddish or Ladino.
Hebrew, so it seemed, had been doomed to be a dead
language like ancient Greek or Latin.

The Haskalah movement, which began at the end of the
eighteenth century, and the national reawakening, the first
signs of which appeared a few decades later, awakened
Hebrew from its long sleep. A whole group of authors arose
in Eastern Europe and began to formulate a Hebrew style.
At the same time, a group led by Eliezer Ben-Yehuda
became active in Jerusalem, its aim being to transform
Hebrew into a spoken language. The Hebrew Language
Committee, which was founded at Ben-Yehudah's initiative
in 1890 and later, after the establishment of the State,
became the Academy for the Hebrew Language, became a
body which labored at implementing the use of Hebrew and
the rational coining of concepts and terms. The daily needs
of those who spoke Hebrew, together with the Hebrew
newspapers and books, whose number kept growing, also
contributed their part.

In our times, Hebrew is the language of Israeli society. New
olim study it in special courses referred to as *ulpanim*, and
even the members of the minorities use it freely. It is
constantly being renewed, both by imports from other
languages as well as by adapting words taken from the
ancient Hebrew sources, as daily life requires it. It has
curses and blessings, street language and the language of
culture. It is used for learned scientific lectures, for writing
lyrics to popular songs, for drafting legal documents and
even for political speeches which may or may not be
interesting. It is used by eleven dailies, hundreds of
periodicals and thousands of new books which are
published each year. Its sounds are heard on the regular
theater programs, in plays of every description – as well as
in films which are created in it.

As the Israeli author, Aharon Amir, said, a few years ago: "If
there is ever ... the possibility of denying, either externally or
internally, the identification of the land now in our hands

Children's books (Above, right) are part and parcel of the Hebrew Revolution. The Hebrew Language Academy is an energetic official institution, the foundations of which were laid by Eliezer Ben-Yehuda (Left, with his wife Hemda) in the 1890s.

with our national way of life (and the limits of this identity), in reality there is no doubt about the total identity of the Hebrew language and the national Hebrew way of life."

Play, O Harp

One of the great days of the Hebrew language came on December 10, 1966, when Shmuel Yosef Agnon, a resident of Jerusalem, stood up in a concert hall in Stockholm in order to receive from the hands of the King of Sweden the Nobel prize for literature for the body of his writings in Hebrew, though many of his works have been translated into other languages. Nor is Agnon the only Israeli writer to be published in translation. Over the years, many Israeli authors and poets have been published abroad, and in Israel itself great efforts are expended in translations into Hebrew.

In the plastic arts, too, there is much artistic ferment. Israel has long been known as a country of music, one of its best-known institutions being the Israel Philharmonic Orchestra. The IPO was founded in 1936, due primarily to the initiative of a brilliant Jewish violinist, Bronislaw Huberman, and to the desire to provide employment for Jewish musicians endangered in Nazi Europe. "The orchestra of this old-new land," Huberman had said, "must serve not only as a source for spiritual uplift which will inspire the people who are re-building this land, but it will prepare the ground for the growth of a musical culture, that will one day yield mankind a supreme composer."

The Philharmonic Orchestra began performing under the baton of the great Arthur Toscanini, and it soon became known throughout the Middle East. Later, it was privileged to perform under the greatest conductors and with the

169

greatest soloists, covering almost every famous musician in the world: Leonard Bernstein, Arthur Rubinstein, Jascha Heifetz, David Oistrakh, Isaac Stern, and many others. It has toured throughout the world, warmed the hearts of Jews in distant corners of the world, and has been labelled, as a result of its tours, "the best ambassador of Israel." It has produced exceptional recordings. It has shaped the pattern of the musical culture of Israeli society. This culture has already produced a number of world-class musicians. The "world-class composer" of which Huberman dreamed, though, is still waiting in the wings.

The Israel Experience is everything mentioned above, as well as Yad Sarah – a volunteer network spread throughout the country which deals with supplying the medical needs of the sick and old.

The Israel Experience is also the Society for the Preservation of Nature – an institution which fights persistently to preserve Israel's natural habitats, and which has already taught the public not to pick endangered flower species.

The Israel Experience is also the Shrine of the Book at the Israel Museum, where the Dead Sea Scrolls are kept. It also includes the Inbal Dance Troupe, which perpetuates the Jewish folk dances of Yemen and other countries. Each year, Israel has its Book Fair, the Israel Festival, and Music in the Upper Galilee.

The Shrine of the Book in the Israel Museum houses the Dead Sea Scrolls - another aspect of the Israeli experience.

The Israel Experience is also a siren which brings all traffic to a halt for a minute of silence in memory of the fallen IDF soldiers, and interminable debates each Friday night about the "situation", and repeated promises that "it'll be fine," and exchanges of curses between drivers of cars, and noisy picnics underneath the trees, and everyone knowing everyone else, and everyone giving everyone else advice, and jokes which circulate throughout the country at lightning speed.

And possibly, more than all of these, the Israel Experience is continuous movement, unceasing ferment, a noisy mosaic: with the drawbacks of a lack of stability, a certain flexibility, resourcefulness in stormy times – and with eternal hope for the reign of peace.

The Jews
and Spain

Some claim that the word Hispania is actually I-Sefania – the Isle of Sefania – reminding us of the fact that it sheltered (safan in Hebrew) the ships that faced Mediterranean storms. Others point to the tombstone, in Sagunto, of Adoniram, King Solomon's finance minister. And there are those, such as Don Isaac Abarbanel in his Bible commentary, who claim that the name Toledo derives from the Hebrew, taltela, "wandering," indicating that Jews exiled from Eretz Israel in the last days of the First Temple reached that city. In the Bible we also find, in the Book of Obadiah, that "the captivity of Jerusalem, which is in Sefarad (the customary Hebrew word for Spain), shall possess the cities of the south," though we do not know exactly what the prophet meant or when the statement was made.

In any event, whether the first Jews arrived there on Phoenician ships or by other means, there can be no doubt at all that there were Jews in Spain in the first century C.E., the evidence being in the works of Josephus, in Paul's Letter to the Romans in the New Testament ("When I take my journey into Spain"), in various places in the Mishna, Talmud and Midrash – as well as on tombstones in the cities of Tarragona and Tortosa.

During the Roman era, the original Jewish settlers of the Iberian peninsula were joined by co-religionists from other places: slaves brought from Judea after the destruction of the Second Temple; immigrants who had fled the East in the wake of rebellions and wars, arriving via North Africa or Italy and Provence; all laying foundations for the Jewish

community which was to exist in Spain for close to 1500 years, one which differed from other Jewish communities in three important ways: its comprehensive flourishing of culture, its unprecedented and unparalleled socio-economic structure, and broad scale Jewish autonomy, complete with a binding judicial system.

From the Emperor to the Caliph

The Jews who lived in Spain during Roman rule were apparently citizens with full rights who engaged in all occupations, including agriculture, maintaining estates (and thus slaves), and were much involved in social and economic life and in close contact with their neighbors. When Christianity was proclaimed the official religion of the Roman Empire (324 C.E.), the condition of the Jews deteriorated; the central government still protected them, but local elements and the church conspired against and tormented them. A church council held in Elvira at the beginning of the fourth century C.E., for example, adopted various resolutions meant to impose restrictions on the Jews, and about a hundred years later bloody fighting broke out between Christians and Jews on the island of Minorca, ending in the burning of the synagogue, the mass slaughter of Jews, and the forced conversion of the survivors.

The Visigoths, who occupied most of Spain in 418 C.E., were at first sympathetic to the Jews, but things began to change in 506, when the first Visigoth laws, which included various anti-Jewish decrees, were published. These restrictions became even more stringent in 587, when the royal court converted from Arian Christianity to Roman Catholicism, persecution reaching a peak in 613. King Sisebut decreed that the Jews had to choose between conversion and expulsion. Some chose the second option, leaving for North Africa, but most of them became Marranos – Crypto-Jews – ostensibly Christian but continuing secretly to practice their Judaism. The fact that the kings and bishops had to introduce decrees against the Jews every few years seems to indicate that the Christian government lacked the power to enforce its own decrees. In any event, it is easy to understand why Spanish Jews were wildly enthusiastic when the Muslim army, under Tarik ibn Ziyad, crossed the Straits of Gibraltar in 711, to occupy the entire country.

The "Crown of Damascus" or Burgos Bible (Left) written in 1260 C.E., an outstanding example of the Castilian style. Next to it a 13th century Bible from northern Spain with one of the earliest Spanish descriptions of the vessels used in the Temple.

Spain now became Al-Andalus, at first part of a mighty Muslim empire whose capital was Damascus, then, from 755 on, a separate kingdom, its capital Cordoba. As far as the Jews were concerned, this was a double revolution. Not only were they permitted to practice their religion openly, strengthen their economic base, and take part in the governing system, but in the changed circumstances they were also able to restore their close ties with the great centers of Judaism, especially Babylon. **Geonim**, the great Torah scholars of Babylon, began to visit Spain, bringing with them manuscripts (which were copied and distributed throughout Spain), established **batei midrash**, regularized the order of the prayers, and aided in founding communities. At the same time, many Jews immigrated to Spain from Europe and North Africa.

Like their more veteran brethren, these immigrants rapidly adopted Arabic, the language of the conquerors, as their tongue, producing many works in this language (some written in Hebrew letters) – a development which also underlined the difference between the Jews and the Christians, who were hostile both to Arabic and the Jews.

In 912, the government in Cordoba fell to Abd Al-Rahman III, who, by seventeen years later proclaiming himself Caliph, completed the break between Muslim Spain and the East. Conditions were now ripe for the transformation of Spain into a major Jewish center, and indeed a Jewish leader of stature was available to accomplish just that. Hisdai ibn Shaprut, a doctor and Torah scholar, had first impressed the Caliph by his translations from Greek and Latin into Arabic. Later, he became a confidant of the Caliph, was entrusted with the kingdom's foreign trade and made an important diplomatic advisor. Among others, he was involved in trading with Sancho, the King of Leon, as a result of which he arranged a peace treaty between Sancho and the Caliph; maintained contacts with Constantine VIII, the Byzantine emperor, and with Otto I, the ruler of the Holy Roman Empire; interceded with Byzantine Princess Helene on behalf of the Jews in Italy; and is reputed to have corresponded with the King of the Khazars, a central Asian people who converted to Judaism about 700 C.E.

As leader of the Jewish community, Hisdai saw that rabbis and Torah scholars were brought to Spain, manuscripts acquired, a magnificent library established, and Jewish thought and creativity in many areas – the Bible, Talmud,

דוש בן לבראט
וירבו מנחם בן סרוק
מזכיריו של חסדאי,
משוררים ובלשנים,
שומעים נרגשים את
אגרתו של חסדאי אל
יוסף, מלך הכוזרים.

בני יהודה אנשי
"גלות ירושלים אשר
בספרד" חשבו
משוררים כבני הלוים,
"וישירו שירות בנעם
בניגון כנורות"

The poet-philosopher Solomon Ibn Gabirol was born in Malaga, lived in Saragossa and died in Barcelona. His birthplace honored him with a sculpture (left) by Read Armstrong. Ibn Gabirol's family came to Malaga via Cordoba. (Left) One of the city's ancient Jewish houses.

poetry and philosophy – fostered and supported, thus laying the foundation for what was to be known as the "Golden Age of Spain," that extended over the eleventh and twelfth centuries.

Philosophers and Poets

This Golden Age was associated with a chain of acclaimed Jewish philosophers such as Bahya ibn Pekuda, whose **Hovat HaLevavot** made a lasting impression on Jewish ethical works thereafter, drawing on many sources, including Muslim mysticism and Arabic neo-platonism, and developing a differentiation between "the duty of the (bodily) organs" (which involves external actions) and "the duty of the hearts" (**hovat halevavot**), related to one's internal life; Yehuda HaLevi, author of the **Kuzari**, whose Aliyah to the Holy Land we have already mentioned above; and Solomon ibn Gabirol, the author of **Mekor Hayyim**, a philosophical treatise originally written in Arabic, which for generations was considered to be a Christian philosophical work, studied in its Latin translation in many monasteries. In its five chapters, which are arranged as a dialogue between a teacher and his student, the nature and form of matter are discussed. The work claims that all people must strive to know the purpose of their having been created; that is the way to cling to the **Mekor Hayyim** – the Fountain of Life – and to avoid death. The three philosophers were also noted poets, among the foremost poets in the history of Jewish and Hebrew poetry, the first to write poetry of a secular nature. They and their colleagues – including Moses Ibn Ezra and Abraham Ibn Ezra – not only wrote about the Creator, about religious faith and the longing for Zion, but also about nature and the world, about beauty, women, wine, etc.

Among the greatest Jewish-Spanish poets was Samuel ben Joseph HaLevi Nargila, known as the Nagid. Born in Cordoba in 993, he was educated in the famous yeshiva of Hanoch ben Moshe there, but also acquired considerable knowledge about Greek philosophy, logic, mathematics and astronomy, as well as mastering many languages. Not surprisingly, in one of his poems he thanks God for "knowing the sciences of the Greeks/ and being wise in the wisdom of the Arabs." At eighteen, he began to involve himself in both

Cordoba's Yehuda Ha-Levi Square commemorates the 12th century poet whose elegaic poem "My heart is in the East and I am at the end of the West" made him famous, as did his prose "The Kuzari."
He also wrote Piyyutim- liturgical poems – such as the one included in the Sarajevo Haggadah (insert).

185

commerce and poetry, taking part in a religious debate with a townsman, Ibn Hazzam, later to become one of the greatest Muslim theologians. After Cordoba was destroyed and the caliphate broken up into smaller states, the Nagid fled to Malaga, afterwards wandering to Granada, where he joined the royal court of King Habus (and later of his son Badis), achieving great success and demonstrating remarkable diplomatic skills. At first he collected taxes among the Jews, but from this moved on to becoming advisor to the Minister of Finance, the Finance Minister himself, and the king's right-hand man. In fact he was so successful that the rulers of neighboring Almeria demanded that he be removed from his position, and viewed the rejection of this demand as a pretext for war against Granada. The Nagid led Granada's army into battle, emerging victorious, a feat he repeated often for the next nineteen years, almost until his death, in battles waged primarily against the kingdom of Seville.

But the minister and general was at the same time a leader of the Jews of Andalusia, as a rabbi, as a teacher of Torah in the **bet midrash**, writing on Jewish law, supporting needy Torah scholars, and maintaining ties with numerous Jewish communities throughout the world. According to the Arab author Ibn Hiyyan, he was "one of the most perfect of men ... He excelled in knowledge, tolerance, ... personal charm, ... self-control and natural courtesy." In the midst of all this, he published a book of poetry entitled **Ben Tehilim**, known as the Diwan, a series of philosophical letters entitled **Ben Kohelet**, and a collection of ethical writings named **Ben Mishlei**.

The Crucible of the Castilian Language

Samuel the Nagid died in 1056, bequeathing his position at court and in the Jewish community to his oldest son Joseph, who ten years later would be killed in an upheaval. As a result of this assassination, other Jews in Granada were killed, and the event may be regarded as the beginning of the decline of the Jewish flowering in Muslim Spain. At that time, the battle over the reconquest of Spain by the Christians had already begun; it was linked to the invasion by the North African Almoravids and Almohads, the resultant instability undermining the tranquility and economic security of the Jews, and subjecting them to difficult conditions. While during the Almoravid era, toward the end of the

Granada, from a window of the Alhambra Palace. (Opposite) Granada was where Samuel Ha-Nagid, poet, Rabbi, statesman and commander – lived; (Above) a wealthy Jew provides for the poor on the eve of Passover, from a 1320 C.E. Haggadah which reached Italy after 1492.

Evidence of the variety of Jewish occupations in Spain: 1-2. Mediecal Surgical instruments and medical texts. 3. Glass paintings of ambassadors. 4. Rabbi Moses Arragel learning about translation from Brother Arias, in a 15th century picture; 5. Jewish musicians; 6. a coin from the time of Pedro the First, whose treasurer was a Jew; the medal awarded to General Amrogio di Spinola (1569-1630) scion of a Marrano family.

eleventh century, Jews still served in the royal court as diplomats and doctors, the more fanatic Almohad era was one of devastation. Entire Jewish communities were destroyed and hundreds of Jews fled northward to escape murder and forced conversion. Some of them settled in the Christian kingdoms, some even went on to Provence – incidentally bringing the Spanish Jewish culture to Jews in other parts of Europe. Among these, a prominent part was played by the Ibn Tibbon and Kimhi families, who translated many Arabic Jewish works into Hebrew, thereby enriching the spiritual life of the Jewish communities.

Translation was also at the center of Jewish activity in Toledo, the city which Alfonso VI of Castile had captured in 1085, and which had become the capital of the kingdom. Within a few years after the conquest, a noted school of Jewish translators was created here – including Judah ben Moses, Samuel HaLevi Abulafia, and Zag el de Toledo – which dealt with translation of works in medicine, philosophy and theology from Arabic to Latin.

Latin, however, was the language of the alien Christian world, the world outside Spain, which aroused antagonism not only among the Jews but also among the Christians of the Iberian

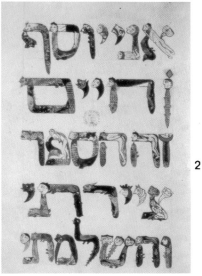

And their vitality:
1. A credit page with the illuminated mane of the calligrapher from the Kennicott Bible, 1476; 2-4. Pages of Spanish Haggadah, showing a cantor, a matza baker and a kosher slaughterer; 5. A Kashrut Seal of the Jewish community of Tarragona, 13th and 14th centuries C.E.

Peninsula. Thus the Toledo school eventually became the Crucible of the Castilian language, and Jews were among the major contributors to it. Fervent admirers of the **Roman** languages, they helped transform these into vehicles for scientific and social expression, pioneering work in the Castilanization of Latin Spain, which was of major significance in shaping the new Spanish nationalism.
The linguistic talents of the Jews, their connections extending beyond the borders of Castile, their realistic assessment of the political constraints under which they lived and which, from the outset, limited them, and the fact that they no longer identified with the Muslims – all these merged to raise their actual status, despite the Church's vehement opposition. So, for example, Joseph HaNasi Ferrizuel, known as Little Cid, was employed as the personal physician and advisor of Alfonso VI – at the same time serving as leader of Castilian Jewry. Another Jewish doctor, Amram ben Isaac, in Toledo when the Christians captured it, was entrusted to negotiate with the Muslim population and to take care of the king's correspondence. The great hero, El Cid, also employed Jewish bankers, treasurers and administrators, as did Ramon Berenguer III, prince of Barcelona (who appointed

The seal of
Nahmanides,
discovered near
Acre:
Opposite: Remains of
a 13th century
synagogue recently
excavated in his
native Gerona. On the
window ledge, the
capital of a pillar
found in
archeological digs in
the Jewish Quarter.
(Insert) The
Nahmanides
Synagogue in
Jerusalem as
envisioned in a 16th
century Hebrew
manuscript.

Sheshet Perfet, the leader of the Jews in Catalonia, as treasurer of the county), and the twelfth century rulers of Aragon.

The fate of Spanish Jews thus changed for the better in the decades of the mid-thirteenth century. Alfonso X, the king of Castile, employed many Jews in his various cultural projects, appointing some as diplomats and tax collectors (for example, Tudrus Abulafia and Don Solomon ibn Zadok, known as Don Culema). Pedro III, the king of Aragon, was aided by Jews in his attempt to extend his kingdom over the eastern shores of Spain and the Mediterranean islands; and in the Crusader kingdom of Valencia, most of whose inhabitants were Muslims, the government was almost entirely in Jewish hands.

Throughout the entire period, however, the law books contained edicts against the Jews, and there was even mention of blood libels, the first of which was launched in 1250. Furthermore, the Church establishment, including the Dominican and Franciscan orders, exerted pressure to undermine the position of the Jews. With the French invasion of 1283, the nobles of Aragon made their support of the king conditional on the removal of Jews from the government, and he acceded to them.

To be precise, even earlier the Dominicans had been engaged in active missionary activity among the Jews. This reached a dramatic peak in 1263, in the famous debate in Barcelona between Pablo Christiani, a converted Jew, representing Christianity, and the celebrated Torah scholar, Rabbi Moses ben Nahman (Nahmanides), representing Judaism. The disputation lasted for four days, each side eventually claiming victory – but the fact that Nahmanides was forced to flee from Spain to Eretz Israel would indicate that he had emerged victorious, and that the governing authorities were very angry. From that time on, the situation of the Jews in Spain began to worsen, though the different kings still offered them protection of some kind, for their own good reasons.

Mysticism and Astronomy

Thirteenth and fourteenth century Catalonia and Castile were the source for many of the fundamentals of kabbalah – Jewish mysticism – including the **Zohar**, a volume which would become one of Judaism's holiest books, written apparently by Moses de Leon. "The Spanish kabbalists,"

wrote the greatest kabbalah scholar of our day, Gershom Scholem, "were not only mystics and bearers of secret teachings, but also served the function of ideologues who protected the folk religion. The kabbalah opposed strongly the trend to make the content of Judaism excessively abstract, as reflected in the philosophy of the rationalists ... It came to save ... the Judaism of the simple believer who was baffled by the new historical conditions ... [As opposed to] the thin layer of wealthy court Jews who were engrossed in the interests and intrigues of politics or of becoming tax farmers ... the kabbalah became the spokesman of poor Torah scholars and pious laymen. Kabbalah's concepts aided these to free themselves of the convolutions of history whose victims they were, based on its unique method ... to return to the era which preceded the creation."

In the fourteenth century, Christian Spain saw the ascent of Shem Tov ben Isaac Ardutiel (Santob de Carrion). At some time between 1355 and 1360 he published **Proverbios Morales**, dedicated to the Castilian king, Pedro I, a work considered to be one of the most decisive influences on Castilian lyric poetry. The central element of the work relates to the golden rule that a person should follow and the relativity of human existence in the world, with a certain melancholy pessimism running through it. Many scholars regard it as the primal source of Spanish literature dealing throughout the generations, with temes of "the tragic meaning of life."

The fourteenth century was also the century of the Jewish astronomers in Spain. The source of this astronomy was the work of the scholar Abraham bar Hiyya HaNasi, who was active in Barcelona in the first half of the twelfth century, and who left after him, among others, his **Book of the Orbits of the Stars** and astronomic tables which were used for calculating the seasons and predicting moon cycles. Among those who followed him were Judah ibn Matkah, author of an encyclopedia (**Midrash Hochma**), much of which was devoted to astronomy; Isaac Yisraeli, whose **Yesod Olam** presented a method for calculating the parallax of the moon; and Judah ben Moses Cohen and Isaac ibn Sa'id, who prepared the **Alphonsine Tables**, upon which Galileo Galilei was to base part of his theories.

A special place must be reserved for Abraham and Judah Crescas, the father and son from Majorca, noted astronomers and cartographers who served the kings of

The statue of Maimonides (right) erected in 1964 in his native Cordova. The little plaza in which it stands is named for Tiberias, where he is buried. A page of his noted "Guide of the Perplexed" (Copenhagen Manuscript, left), decorated by a drawing of an astronomer holding an astrolabe up for his students.

Aragon. In 1376 they prepared the famous **Mapmundi**, a map of the world, that, for the first time, incorporated Marco Polo's discoveries, receiving in partial payment the right to appoint ritual slaughterers for the Jewish community. Abraham Zacuto too was an important astronomer, who worked under the patronage of the bishop of Salamanca and was a professor in the university of that city. Zacuto, who wrote **HaHibbur HaGadol** on astronomy, was also the inventor of the brass astrolabe that replaced the wooden model, greatly simplifying navigation. He also prepared astronomical tables that improved on the **Alphonsine Tables**, aiding two famous explorers: Columbus in his famous voyage to the New World, and Vasco de Gama when he sailed to circumnavigate Africa. Columbus even learned from one of these tables that there would be a moon eclipse at a certain time, and he used this information as a threat to the residents of the Caribbean islands, claiming that he would steal the moon from them if they harmed him or his men. In fact, it can be said that Columbus' voyage could not have taken place without the work of Zacuto and the Jewish

astronomers who preceded him.

One further comment in this connection: it is regarded by many scholars as quite likely that Columbus himself came from a Spanish Jewish family that had moved to Genoa due to religious persecution. They point, for example, and also to the fact that he postponed his departure from August 2nd, 1492 (the major Jewish fast of **Tisha B'Av**, commemorating the destruction of both Temples in Jerusalem) to the next day.

The Expulsion

Either way, three days before Columbus departed, the last Jews crossed the Spanish borders, expelled from Spain by Ferdinand and Isabella. Such was the tragic culmination of a process begun at the end of the fourteenth century. In 1357, Samuel HaLevi of Toledo had still been influential enough to build his famed synagogue in that city (later it was converted into the El Transito church), but by 1391 major pogroms against the Jews broke out in Seville – encouraged by the Church – and soon spread throughout the country. About a third of Spain's Jews were killed; a similar number forced to convert; and many others expelled to North Africa. "The New Christians," not assimilated into the Christian society, still did whatever they could to observe their faith in private. The problem of the Marranos increased not only their tribulation, but that of the Jews in general, the latter being suspected of influencing their former co-religionists. The Jews, led first by Hisdai ibn Crescas and afterwards by Don Isaac Abarbanel and the chief rabbi, Abraham Senior, tried to reorganize their communities, and for a while, in the mid-fifteenth century, there was even a certain improvement in their condition. At the same time, the efforts of the Marranos to be fully accepted by Christian society increased. But other factors – both political and economic – were at work, ultimately contributing to deterioration in the situation.

In 1449, rebellious Christians in Toledo, concerned with their own economic interests, had a law passed forbidding senior government positions from being given to any of the "New Christians." Twenty years later Isabella, Queen of Castile, married Ferdinand, King of Aragon; with the unification of the kingdom, warnings were heard to the effect that this merger would not succeed unless and until a solution was found to the problem of the New Christians. At the urgent request of the Spanish royal family, Pope Sixtus IV ordered that the

Above: The decorated first page of Columbus' report to the Spanish authorities on his first voyage, at the time of the Expulsion.

Preceding pages: a modern mural showing an argument on a Toledo street between Maimonides' followers and his opponents. (Below left) The first page of an early copy of "The Guide"; (Below right) a map of the firmament with ten "spheres" or "divine emanations," from a 14th century copy of the Book of Zohar, the major Kabbalistic text. (Insert) A view of Toledo.

"Council of the Inquisition" be established to investigate instances of heresy – and to uproot them. The Inquisition began enthusiastically to fulfill its task, especially after Tomas de Torquemada, confessor to the queen, was made its head. The members of the Inquisition gladly accepted anonymous information, eagerly latched on to the most tenuous of leads, forced detainees to confess to sins they had not committed, engaged in barbaric means of torture, and burned many at the stake.

The fact the Jews were expelled from Andalusia in 1483 so that they would not be able to influence the Marranos was a confession of the Inquisition's failure, but also a most dangerous precedent. The king and queen were then pre-occupied by their war against Granada, the last Muslim stronghold on Spanish soil, with no time to deal with the Jews whose money they badly needed of conduct the war. But when Granada fell to the Christians at the beginning of 1492 and the Reconquest was completed, these reasons were no longer valid. Furthermore, a burst of religious and political fervor was directed to concluding the "External

Reconquest" with an "Internal Reconquest" - against the Jews, the only group that had not surrendered to the rule of united Christian Spain. On March 31, 1492, the expulsion order was signed in Granada, and at the beginning of May that year, when all attempts to prevent it had been defeated, it was publicly proclaimed.

The Jews were ordered to leave Spain, almost penniless, and within three months – unless they agreed to convert. Some 200,000 accepted the bitter alternative. Only ten thousand chose the second. Thus, shamefully, a historical era which had lasted close to 1,500 years drew to a close.

The Jews and Spain

The expulsion was a terrible blow to the Jews – and to Spain. The "Catholic Kings" evidently hoped that most Jews would convert, thus marking a major religious and political achievement for them while not depriving the government of Jewish funds and talents. Instead, just at the time that Spain was embarking on its greatest imperialistic era, it sustained a major loss, both economically and intellectually. A senior official in the court of Sultan Bayazid, who opened the gates

Horse-shoe shaped arches (Right), in a Toledo Jewish home formed a familiar motif in the architecture of Jewish quarters throughout Spain; a page of a Barcelona Haggadah which arrived in Italy via Bologna, in 1459. (Below) A key ring with the star of David unearthed during a dig in the Old Jewish Quarter of Gerona.

of the Ottoman Empire to the Jews expelled from Spain, put the question succinctly: "This Spanish king, who impoverishes his country in order to enrich it, is he to be considered a wise or discerning ruler?" he asked.

Truth to tell, the expulsion did not mean that Spain had lost all the Jews. Later, a great Spanish historian would state that "from the king down, no one can claim with surety that Jewish blood does not flow in his veins; this is the truer when we deal with our upper classes." In other words, many converts remained in Spain, occupying high positions. These included Luis de Santangel, whose influence on Ferdinand and Isabella was decisive in their backing of Columbus; Fernando de Rojas, who wrote **La Celestina**, the greatest Spanish work after **Don Quixote**; the founders of Spanish mysticism, Juan Delacroix and Juan de Avila; the philosophers Leon Habern, Alfonso de Samorra and Alonzo de Madrigal; the physicians Francesco Villalobos and Christobal Acosta; evidently also the most outstanding woman in Spanish history, Saint Theresa of Avila; and Diego Leons, the second general of the Jesuit order.

Spain, which had expelled its Jews and avowed its intent to be rid of them, remained poor – and also barred, as a result of its own decrees and deeds, from any future

Descendants of Marranos played important roles in Spanish society. Luis Mercado (Left), King Philip II's physician, was far more fortunate than many other Marranos, burnt at the stake in the Inquisition's auto-da-fe executions, depicted (Right) in Pedro Berruqueta's painting.

PHILOSOPHIE
D'AMOVR
DE M. LEON
HEBREV:

Contenant les grands & hauts poinctz, defquels elle traite, tant pour les chofes Morales & Naturelles, que pour les diuines & fupernaturelles.

Traduitte d'Italien en François, par le Seigneur du Parc, Champenois.

D · C · L ·

A LYON,
BENOIST RIGAVD.
M. D. XC V.

developments which might relate to the Jews. Many years later, in 1869, in a vehement debate held in the Spanish parliament, the Liberal leader, Emilio Castelar, spoke of "the great Jewish minds now illuminating the world, which might have shone forth here in Spain had we not expelled our Jews," and offered the example of Baruch Spinoza, "a child of Spanish parents," in whose reflected glory Spain was unable to bask because of its intolerance. The same was true, he said, for Benjamin D'Israeli, another distinguished Jew of Spanish origin. "By having deprived us of the presence of the Jews," he concluded, "you have deprived us of infinite names which could have been a credit to Spain." Those who were expelled scattered throughout the world. More than half of them fled first to Portugal, only to be exposed there, in 1497, to a new expulsion order. Tens of thousands landed in North Africa, particularly in Morocco, and many came to Italy. Others, as mentioned above, streamed to the Ottoman Empire, settling throughout it – in Eretz Israel, in Iraq, in Egypt, and in the Balkans. And there were some who set sail for the New World to found new Jewish congregations in Recife, Brazil, in Curacao and in New Amsterdam, which would later become New York.

With them they carried spiritual treasures created in Spain, first and foremost the works of Maimonides. They and their descendants preserved the kabbalah, the Sephardic liturgy, and the unique Judeo-Espanol tongue, Ladino, pre-Cervantes and pre-Columbian Spanish; for the language which the Spanish conquistadors carried with them to the New World was that which the Spanish Jews took with them into exile, to serve them as a reminder of Spain and its landscape, of the pleasant life in that land and of the golden era which preceded persecution and expulsion.

It was in this language that the folk **romanceros**, the purest expression of their collective identity, were written. Hundreds of years after the expulsion, those Spanish **romanceros** echoed in the Jewish quarters of Salonika, Sofia, Bucharest, Sarajevo, Belgrade, Izmir, Jerusalem, Hebron, Damascus, Aleppo, Cairo, Tangiers and Alexandria. The Spanish traveller, Domingo de Tual, who reached Aleppo in 1634, was surprised to find hundreds of Jewish homes where the songs of Spanish poets of that era were to be heard along with fourteenth and fifteenth century **romanceros**. They also included songs with linguistic innovations, as well as echoes and the flavor of the life of the new Spanish diaspora.

The expulsion burned in the hearts of the Jews like a furnace, but it had not totally obliterated strong emotions. Part of the hearts of those who had been expelled remained "at the end of the west," the name for Spain coined by the poet Yehuda HaLevi, or it may be more accurate to say that "the end of the west" remained engraved in their hearts wherever they went.

Israel
2000 Plus

שלום

PILU

"From the day of the Temple's destruction," so states the Talmud, "the gift of prophecy was taken away from the prophets and given to simpletons and infants." In other words, in the Jewish tradition, prophecy is not to be taken seriously; wise men will distance themselves from it. And indeed, totally unpredictable events which have shaken the world over the past years would appear to support this thesis, as does the huge progress in science and technology which, in the twentieth century, has opened up for mankind undreamed of vistas. Furthermore, this has to be coupled with our concern that various global processes – ecological and other – may be such that mankind may simply be unable to control them.

Nevertheless, despite the surprises, disappointments and uncertainties we have known, let us attempt a sketch of Israel in the not-remote future, in the 21st century.

The Road to Peace

In the final section of the declaration of the establishment of the State of Israel – presented in the midst of a bitter war and only a few hours before the threatened invasion of the newborn state by the armies of the Arab states – we read: "We extend our hand to all neighbouring states and their peoples in an offer of peace and good neighbourliness, and appeal to them to establish bonds of cooperation and mutual help with the sovereign Jewish people settled in its own land. The State of Israel is prepared to do its share in the common effort for the advancement of the entire Middle East." For a long time, the extended hand was rejected.

Arab swords have not been returned to their scabbards. In the forty-five years that have passed, war has broken out time after time. But the hope that the Israel of the 21st century will live in peace stubbornly persists, anchored in the deeply rooted Jewish tradition which glorifies peace, and has turned the word **shalom** ("peace") into the common Israeli greeting.

This hope stems from the very fact that the State has battled time after time for its existence, and has shown that brute force cannot overcome it.

This hope rests on the assumption that the Middle Eastern region is now in the midst of sobering up from various delusions and is coming to grips with reality, and thus may make possible a halt to the arms race and may bring about the acceleration of moderate forces.

This expectation is also nurtured by the changes that have taken place recently on the international front, with the collapse of the Iron Curtain and the replacement of mutual deterrence by mutual disarmament, with the new possibility of a common front against explosive socio-economic tensions and the battle against disease, pollution and fanaticism which do not recognize national boundaries. The Middle East is not what it once was. And in the new situation, there is a good possibility for the fulfillment of the prophetic vision: "They will beat their swords into ploughshares and their spears into pruning hooks."

A vision never abandoned, it has several times seemed about to be fulfilled. The talks held on Rhodes at the beginning of 1949 come to mind: the battles of the War of Independence had begun to die down, the delegates of Israel and Egypt met to discuss an armistice, as an interim stage between the cease-fire at the front and permanent peace. They argued and debated for six difficult weeks, reached an agreement, signed it, and, doing so, paved the way for similar agreements with Jordan, Lebanon and Syria. The introductions to these agreements state that they are based on "a desire to advance the return of peace to Eretz Israel." The UN mediator, US diplomat Dr. Ralph Bunche, would be awarded the Nobel Peace Prize a year later for his efforts. But peace itself was delayed. More than eighteen years passed with Israel isolated from its neighbors, its isolation accompanied by Arab boycott. Neither people nor goods crossed the borders unless in military operations; Israeli Arabs were unable to undertake the pilgrimages to

The three partners to the Camp David Accords (From left to right) Menachem Begin, Jimmy Carter, Anwar Sadat. (Insert) Checking passports at the Allenby Bridge – Israel's policy of keeping the Jordan River bridges open came in the wake of the Six Day War.

Mecca; no regional development and cooperation was possible. The young State was surrounded by walls of hostility.

One wall began to crack following the Six Day War of 1967. In Khartoum, the capital of Sudan, the Arab rulers decided on their famous "Three Noes," forbidding contact with Israel or recognition of it – but along the Jordan river the bridges were opened for two-way traffic, which signified the beginning of a partial breakdown in the alienation, though it was non-political and not in the open. Across those bridges, Israeli goods began to move into the Arab world, and here and there Arab patients began coming to Israel for hospitalization and surgery.

The second Nobel Peace Prize to be associated the Middle East was awarded in 1978 – to Israeli prime minister Menahem Begin and Egyptian president Anwar Sadat, who confirmed the Camp David Accords as an introduction to the peace treaty between their two countries. The agreement

Opposite: An artistic urban vision: "White City" by Dani Karavan, a sculpture in Givatayim, near Tel Aviv.

Below: The Madrid Conference at the end of 1991 marked a new stage of the Middle Eastern peace process. New life in the shadow of Scud missiles: gas masks in an Israeli maternity ward during the Gulf War.

itself was signed in Washington on March 26, 1979, a year and a half after Sadat's dramatic trip to Jerusalem and his address to the Israelis from the Knesset rostrum. The two sides, it was decided, would recognize and respect "each other's sovereignty, territorial integrity and political independence," and agreed that "the normal relationship established between them will include diplomatic recognition, with economic and cultural relations, termination of economic boycotts and discriminatory barriers to the free movement of people and goods." In February 1980, ambassadors were exchanged. Israeli tourists began to visit Egypt, Israeli experts founded agricultural training centers in Egypt, Egyptian oil began to flow to Israel.

The peace treaty resulted in Egypt's expulsion from the Arab League – for a few years. Slowly, most of the rulers of the Arab states began to come to terms with changing conditions. At the beginning of the 1990's, the global peace process (linked to the collapse of the Soviet Union) and the Gulf War worked together to grant new momentum to

melting the ice between Israel and its neighbors. The fact that the Arab states could no longer rely on Moscow to arm (and incite) them, along with the memory of the Scud missiles that had been fired from western Iraq at both Saudi Arabia's Riyad as well as Tel Aviv, intensified a sense of the need for a political settlement to bring a new era to the region.

It was against this background that the peace conference, eventually convened in Madrid on October 31, 1991, was born, followed by bilateral talks in Washington and multilateral talks in Moscow. In all three cities there were direct negotiations between Israel and its neighbors, and the cracks in the wall of hostility grew. It may be safe to assume that the wall will crumble completely during the next century. Last but not least, a Middle-eastern economic community seems now to be more than a dream.

The Hamster and the Computer

Peace will enable the Middle East to enjoy the fruits of Israel's scientific achievements. This science was born at the very beginning of the Zionist movement, with many of the movement's founders being scholars whose Zionism was not divorced from scientific involvement. They had experienced – to a greater or lesser extent, some directly and others indirectly – the **numerus clausus** that limited the percentage

The particle accelerator at the Weizmann Institute of Science, the research center founded by Israel's first President, the noted chemist Dr. Chaim Weizmann.

of Jews at European institutes of higher learning; they understood or sensed that national revival depended on a series of rational processes, and they wished to support it with their own "personal" rationalism. They realized, possibly intuitively, that it is man's spirit which creates material resources. Later, Dr. Chaim Weizmann, Israel's first president, would say: "I feel sure that science will bring to this land both peace and a renewal of its youth."

At the very first Zionist Congress, in 1897, a resolution was submitted, "to engage in intense activity for ... the establishment of a higher school of learning (a school for Torah, science and labor)." Two presidents of the Zionist Organization – the botanist Otto Warburg and the chemist Chaim Weizmann – were noted scientists. As early as 1921, the Zionist movement had established an experimental agricultural station, and in 1925 the Hebrew University in Jerusalem was founded. Incidentally, the first lecture, given before the official inauguration, was by Albert Einstein, on the Theory of Relativity. And even if most of those present were unable to fathom the lecture as such, there was no one who did not understand the impassioned declaration of the chairman: "Come up, Professor Einstein, to the rostrum which has been waiting for you for two thousand years." The experimental station and the university, as well as the Technion in Haifa and the Sieff Institute in Rehovot, created a

Israeli scientists have contributed substantially to today's revolutionary genetic research: molecular models in Weizmann Institute labs.

scientific infrastructure for "the State in the making," cultivating scientists, developing methods and technologies suited to the local conditions, producing medicines and fertilizers, insect-resistant plants, totally new laboratory animals (like the Golden Hamster), means for exploiting the resources of the Dead Sea, and new innovations in theoretical physics – as well as explosives which helped in the defense of the **Yishuv**.

Since 1948, a broad scale scientific system has developed, with three major branches: the academic (including the Hebrew University in Jerusalem, the Haifa Technion, the Weizmann Institute, Tel Aviv University, Bar Ilan University, Ben-Gurion University in Beersheba, and Haifa University); government civilian research, comprising a series of institutes responsible to various government ministries, among them the Agricultural Research Administration, the Oceanological Institute, research laboratories of Israel Chemicals, the Geological Institute, the Geophysical Institute, the Meteorological Service, etc.; and, finally, security-oriented research, embracing the Weapons Development Authority (Raphael) among others. To these can be added numerous laboratories in different industrial concerns and medical centers, colleges of all kinds, and Everyman's University. The list of achievements of Israeli science is too long and too varied to be given here. A glance will show such items as pioneering work in the computer field, which, in the early 1950's, yielded "Weizac," one of the first computers in the world, and which took the country into the computer age; seminal research in the physics of elementary particles, utilizing some of the largest particle accelerators in the world in multinational projects; an innovative method of creating heavy oxygen (and a facility supplying 90% of the world's consumption of this isotope); the founding of the science of liquids (rheology); the development of affinity chromatography, used for the separation and location of substances essential for biological processes and which play a significant role in genetic engineering; technologies for the fixation of enzymes, incorporated into various biotechnological industries; a "surgical gun," based on laser beams; experiments in chromosomal engineering which produces high-yielding wheat strains; the discovery of synthetic materials which inhibit sclerosis; the original production of medicines based on Interferon; the planning

State-of-the-art printing systems, products of Israeli development and manufacture, are to be found all over the world.

and building of mini remote-piloted vehicles and of a communications satellite; the improving of cloud-seeding devices to increase rainfall.

Behind this non-exhaustive list are literally thousands of scientists whose research is published in international journals, whose lectures are heard at major international conferences, and whose laboratories attract colleagues from all over the world. Some of them have been awarded highly prestigious prizes: Ephraim Katzir (the fourth president of the State) – the Japan prize (in biotechnology); Yuval Ne'eman (who served for several years as the Minister of Science and Energy) – the Einstein Prize (physics); Chaim Leib Pekeris – the Vetlesen Prize (considered equivalent to the Nobel Prize for earth sciences); Leo Sachs – the Wolf Prize (medicine); Meir Wilchek, Joshua Yortener and Raphael Levin – the Wolf Prize (chemistry). They and others belong to such bodies as the US National Academy of Science and Britain's Royal Society.

Eminent scientists at the helm: biochemist Prof. Ephraim Katzir, Israel's fourth President, 1973-1978 (Above); physicist Yuval Ne'eman, Minister of Science, 1982-1984, 1990-1992.

With the Face to the Future

It is of course hard to forecast scientific developments and even harder to determine the directions Israeli scientists take which may gain them worldwide status. Everyone understands that scientific innovation today depends not only on fertile minds, but also, if not primarily, on financial resources, on costly equipment, and on complex often far-flung team work. At the same time, the Israeli research community will clearly continue to seek, and find, unique ways to express its ability and originality. Many such will probably be found in the realm of biotechnology. Chaim Weizmann was a pioneer in this area during World War I, when he developed a bacteriological method for producing acetone from vegetable matter, and Israeli scientists have long been involved in similar work, based on fundamental research (unknown to Weizmann and his generation) and on new information. These scientists have travelled from academe to sophisticated industries, and will probably chalk up achievements for themselves in the development and production of medicinal preparations – ranging from hormones to aid in the overcoming of congenital problems to fumigation materials which will not pollute the atmosphere. There is reason to hope that these achievements will also find expression in Israel's economy.

Other field also relate, at least potentially, to energy. Israel is

blessed with abundant sunlight and, by its nature, is a convenient place for studies in the harnessing of solar energy for man's use. The Dead Sea has been considered, for some time, to be a massive solar pool, and there are already sites in the Negev being used for experiments in techniques of energy storage. Add to this the thermal turbines developed in Israel and exported throughout the world, the "sun tower" functioning in Rehovot for the past few years, and the idea of the "heat carrier" which has occupied Israeli scientists for some time – and you have a recipe for intense activity in this area.

Energy research is also required for desalination of sea water. It is true that the Middle East lies atop large quantities of oil, but it has suffered, throughout history, from shortages of water. A constantly growing population calls not only for the reasonable utilization of available water but no less for development of new water sources, i.e., first and foremost, conversion of sea water for human use. At present, this is carried out with only small quantities of water and at a high price, but it is logical to foresee the development and construction of safe thermonuclear power stations. This, too, is among the great challenges of Israeli science as it enters the 21st century.

A Strategic Question

The building of such reactors, like the fair allocation of the water resources of the Middle East, is, of course, conditional

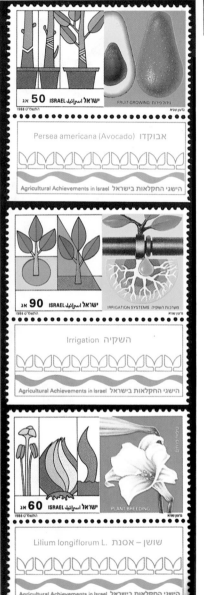

Israel's science-based agriculture as reflected in 1988 Israeli stamps. From top to bottom: fruit growing; flower cultivation; irrigation systems.

on regional agreements. If there is no peace, if Middle Eastern states must continue to invest much of their national incomes and efforts in the readying and maintaining of war machines, if tension remains an identifying mark of the region, there can be no way of effectively utilizing existing water supplies or building the reactors necessary for desalinating sea water. On the other hand, if peace exists, it will alleviate the water resource problem, and will, in turn, contribute to the alleviation of other friction points. In a peaceful Middle East, it will be possible to undertake major, multinational ecological efforts to deal with pollutants, preserve air quality, and ensure the proper balance between man and his environment. This kind of Middle East will be able to exploit its human potential and accumulated knowledge for the benefit of all concerned.

Take, for example, medicine. Today, the Israeli medical system is the subject of fierce public debate, but an impressive number of important achievements are to its credit: it has offered comprehensive medical care to virtually all Israeli citizens. Israel's medical services are among the most advanced in the world. Their advancement made possible the elimination in Israel of diseases such as malaria, tuberculosis and trachoma, though these still claim their victims in developing countries. This system, which at present suffers from a surplus of trained personnel and which has to invest large sums of money in order to preserve its quality, can only be exploited properly if it is not limited solely to the Israeli population. It has the ability, if peace should be declared, to service many of the neighboring countries, and possibly reach out even beyond these. This, too, may be a direction Israel will take in coming decades.

Such medical development may, in effect, be considered to be one of Israel's advanced industries. To be more precise, it will play a significant role as part of a proper national strategy which will be of key importance in the foreseeable future, in order to realign the Israeli economy in general along the lines of the specialization without which there can be no economic thrust. Future Israeli industry will have to be based on automation and robotics, to maintain close links with the innovations of basic research, to develop its own advanced laboratories, and to concentrate on products calling for know-how – rather than for raw materials or energy. Will it be able to do so? Existing Israeli companies

"Jerusalem the Golden," originally a piece of jewelry bought by Rabbi Akiva for his devoted wife; later, the name of an Israeli popular song that became the "anthem" of the Six Day War; now, a fashionable new Israeli export item, modelled here by Israeli singer Ofra Hazah.

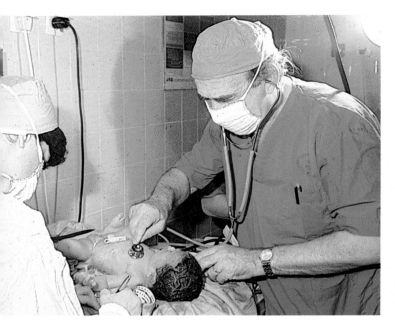

Out of Zion Shall Go Forth Medicine: Israel's first test-tube baby (left); and a made-in-Israel computerized body scanner.

producing advanced typesetting systems, computer chips, improved industrial blades, electro-optical equipment and communications equipment show that this is well within the realm of the possible. But much, of course, depends on the human factor and on socio-political aspects, on the will of the government, and on its ability to determine priorities and adapt legislation and regulation to changing circumstances. Israel of the decades ahead will also have to invest much in education at all levels and in developing cultural creativity of various kinds. This is not a simple requirement, since it is based on the need to rectify inequities of the past, on the need for quality manpower in an advanced economy, and on the desire to preserve the central place of the State of Israel in the lives of the Jewish people. As in the past, so too at present and assumedly in the future as well, the Jewish people throughout the world are "the People of the Book." Their numbers in academia, in advanced economic activity, in literature and philosophy, in the formulation of new social patterns, are far higher, in terms of percentages, than those of the overall world population. If Israel will not fit into such a pattern, it will be difficult for the Jewish State to maintain a dialogue and ties with the rest of the Jewish people, who, in the final analysis, are its most devoted allies. There, too, the challenge is clear but there are many question marks.

The Forecasts of the Past

In the opening we have already stated that one cannot easily

forecast what is to happen in the 21st century. This being the case, let us return to a forecast made at the beginning of this century, and see how it fared. In his book **Altneuland**, Theodor Herzl attempted to describe, from the perspective of 1902, the new society to arise in Eretz Israel within twenty years. He saw the old-new country as one in which western science prevails, but is nevertheless firmly linked to the entire eastern world. **Altneuland** also mentions a solution to the problem of the Holy Places of the three religions, health spas as a serious industry, underground electric cables in the cities, compulsory education laws which include international tours, and a vision of a research institute whose director declares to young guests of his institute: "Science has taught us that we can make life anywhere in the world more pleasant and healthier.... Thanks to young people with technical training and to entrepreneurs, we have brought here all known industries.... In modern life there are reciprocal relationships between industry and agriculture.... One depending on the other. But what is needed are the initiative and know-how. I, as you see me, even though I am no more than a learned donkey, work for industry and agriculture."

Following this, the scholar leads his guests to the laboratory, where Herzl depicts the following scene for us:

"'I work here.'

'Doing what, if one may ask?' Friedrich wished to know.

The scholar's eyes became dreamy.

'The development of Africa!' The visitors thought that they had not heard properly, or that the scholar's mind was going.

... 'You said: the development of Africa?'

...'Yes ... There is another terrible national problem that has not yet been solved; only a Jew can appreciate the depth of the tragedy. That is the problem of the blacks ... That is why I work on the development of Africa. All peoples deserve their own homeland because then they will be more pleasant to one another, and they will love one another and understand one another.'"

And a few pages later, in his "Epilogue," Herzl writes: "If you do not will it, it is and will remain a fairy-tale, this story that I have told you."

Picture Credits

The Ministry of Defense Publishing House (MOD) and Massada Publishing Ltd. has made every effort possible to locate the copy right holders of the photographs. We apologize to any photographer, private individual or body, or other institution whose photographs have been incorporated into this publication, without appropriate acknowledgement.

MUSEUMS AND ARCHIVES

Antiquities Authority/Photographs' Archive: 12 (photograph: Israel Museum), 56, 62 (top).
Bayerische Library, Munich: 195 (bottom).
Beth Hatefutsot: 37 (left), 38, 44, 46, 139 (top right) - courtesy of Malkah Dassah, Givatayim; 182 - Photo Archives, Postcard, 174-175 (top) - permanent exhibition, photographer Yaakov Brill, 183 (bottom) - Permanent Exhibition, 188 (center) - permanent exhibition; 191 - Photo Archives, Victor Laredo Collection; 194 (bottom) - permanent exhibition, 194-195 - permanent exhibition photographer Yaakov Brill, 198 (right & center) - Photo Archives, Victor Laredo Collection.
Bibliothèque Nationale, Paris: 36, 82 (top), 178, 181 (right), 188 (top left), 188 (bottom center).
Bodleian Library, Oxford: 189 (top left), 194-195 (bottom).
British Museum, London: 81, 174 (bottom), 187 (top), 188 (bottom, right), 189 (right; top center), 198 (left).
Central Zionist Archive: 137, 149.
David City Excavation Mission: 62.
Det Kongelige Bibliotek, Kobenhavn: 37 (right); 193 (right).
Gemeeint Museum, The Hague, Holland: 39.
Gorki (Nizhni Novgorod) Museum: 28.
Government Press Office: 50, 96 (photograph: Klugger), 98, (left), 99, 134 (second bottom, left); 135, second bottom, right), 140 (photograph: Klugger),141, 142 (top), 145 (photograph: Klugger), 147 (bottom, photograph: Klugger), 148 (Photograph: Klugger), 151 (photograph: Klugger), 155, 158, 160 (left), 165 (1, 4), 170, 209, 210, 216, 217 (top).
I.D.F. Archive: 100 (bottom).
Institute for Labor Movement Rescarch, in memory of Pinchas Lavon, Tel-Aviv: 97 (right), 102, 145 (top).
Israel Antiquities Research Society: 54-55.
Israel Museum, Jerusalem: 14-15, 17 21, 22 (left), 25, 30 (top), 60 (Eiran Laor Collection), 48, 61 (bottom), 73,

74, 75 (bottom), 80, 81 (top), 84, 87, 90 (right), 109, 114, 139 (center), 140 (top left), 164, 190, 202-3 (bottom), 219 (bottom), 221, 222 (top).
John Rylando University Library, Manchester: 189 (bottom center).
Keren Kayemet Le'Israel Archive: 100 (top - photograph: Melavski), 146.
Library of Hungarian Academy of Science, Kaufman Collection, Budapest: 200 (right).
Madrid Palacio de Liria, The Duke of Alba's Library: 188 (right).
Maritime Museum, Haifa: 188 (bottom, large coin).
Musej Czrada, Sarajevo: 185 (left), Facsimile photocopy.
Museo del Prado, Madrid: 199 (right).
Museum of Art, Named after Haim Attar, Ein Kharod, 12
National and University Library Jerusalem, Manuscript Department: 42, 83, 178 (bottom), 181 (left), 189 (bottom, left), 191 (bottom), 197.
National Library, Lisbon: 179.
Nature Reserve Authority: 20 (photographer: Jossi Leon).
N.Y. Academy of Medicine: 199 (El Libro de la Peste - front page).
Rijksmuseum Amsterdam: 31.
Seo de Urgel Archiv der Kathedrale: 33.
Spain Avila, Archivo Historico Provincial: 200 (top left).
Schoken Institute, Jerusalem: 20 (bottom).
Staats Und Universitäts Bibliothek, Hamburg: 70.
Tel Aviv Museum: 40, 103
Theological Seminary, New York: 26.

PHOTOGRAPHERS:

Shlomoh Arad: 125.
Dan Arnon: 119, 122.
Micha Bar-Am: 71, 93, 135 (center).
Meir Ben-Dov: 62 (bottom), 82, 111, 112 (left), 113, 115, 117 (left), 122 (top), 124, 131.
Herbert Bishco: 52, 57, 77.
Alex Gal: 161 (top).
Mike Ganor, Tel Aviv: 176, 177, 180 (right, left), 184 (right, left), 193 (left), 196.
Gottex, Jerusalem of Gold, Gottex '92 Collection, Design: Lea Gottlieb, Photographer: Ben-Lam, Photo: Ofra Haza, The International Israeli Singer: 219.
Chanokh Gutmann: 161.
Abraham Hai: 16, 41, 52 (bottom), 61 (top), 65 (left), 67, 95 (top), 112 (right), 165.
Jack Khanani: 89.
Shaul Khomski: 59 (top).
Photography: Yakis Kidron, Optrotec, Design: Ilan Molcho: 204.
Alex Lieback: 159 (right).
Reuven Milone: 129 (bottom), 217 (bottom), 218 (top), 221 (top).

Eliyah On: 202-3.
Orpan Ltd - Multimedia Communications: 134 (third bottom left), 135 (third bottom right).
Uzi Paz: 136.
The Philatelic Service - Post Office Authority: 30, 32, 144, 205, 218.
Shmuel Rakhmani: 162-163.
Riki Rosen: 156 (right), 157.
Nettah Rosenblatt/The Information Center: 23, 58, 65, 77, 116, 126, 134 (top right first and second top), 135 (right - first top, bottom), 135 (left - three bottom photographs), 173.
Yossi Rotem, Design: Rubi Showel: 205.
Scitex Corporation Ltd.: 215.
Duby Tal (Photography), Moni Haramati (Flight), "Albatross" (Aerial Flight): 1, 2-3, 4-5, 6-7, 8-9, 12-13, 29, 56, 64, 75, 85 (top), 106-107, 133-134, 147, 151 (bottom), 165 (5), 167 (top left), 167 (bottom left), 167 (top left), 167 (bottom right), 171 (top right), 171 (bottom), 172, 185 (right), 187, 194-195, 211, 222 (bottom).
Michael Tal: 139 (bottom).
Tel Aviv University: 214.
The Weizman Institute of Science, Photography Laboratory, Rehovot: 212, 213.
Yavneh Publishing Ltd.: 68.
Zackai Shai: 120, 128, 129 (top), 136 (top), 142 (top left), 142 (bottom), 167 (top right).
Zamir Yehoshua: 134 (top second right, left second top, bottom, right and left), 135 (top left), 152 (right), 152 (left), 153.

ARTISTS AND COLLECTORS

Max Berger (Vienne): 90 (left).
Bineth Gallery, Tel Aviv: 45.
Yehoshua Brandstatter courtesy of Tzillie Brandstatter: 92, 154.
Yitzhak Einhorn, Tel Aviv: 22 (right - photography: Ran Erdah), 78.
Nahum Gutmann: 85 (bottom).
Kan, Al Pnei Haaddama (Here, on Earth): 139 (top left).
Shmuel Katz, Gaaaton: 159 (left).
Alef-Beit Book - Rhymes Levin Kippnis, Art: Z. Rabban, Modan Publishing Ltd., Tel Aviv: 169.
Abbel Pan: 24 (courtesy of lethiel Pan).
Reuven Rubin, Ayalah Zachs - Abramov Collection: 95.
Design: David Tartakover: 206.
Tel Aviv Museum of Arts; Dvir Publishing Ltd., Painting With Light - The Photographic Aspect in the Work of E.M. Lilien, Design & Editing: Ornah & Micha Bar-Am. 117 (right), 119 (bottom), 125 (center).
Mr. and Mrs. Philips Weglemann Collection N.Y.: 104.
Josef Zaritzki, Shyah Yariv Collection, Tel Aviv: 127.

All Rights Reserved to:
Massada Ltd. and MOD Publishing House, Israel

Color separations: Scanli Ltd. Israel
Typesetting: El-ot Ltd. Israel
Printing and binding: Peli Printing Works, Israel

ISBN 965-05-0629-2